Keto Diet Instant Pot Cookbook For Rapid Weight Loss And A Better lifestyle

Top 101 Quick, Easy & Delicious Low Carb Ketogenic Diet Instant Pot Recipes(Including 14 Days Fat Loss Meal Plan)

By Frank Donald

D1502331

Table of Contents

Introduction

Hello friend! This is Frank Donald. Firstly, I would like to congratulate and thank you you for choosing this book, **"Keto Diet Instant Pot Cookbook For Rapid Weight Loss And A Better lifestyle"**.

This book suits for people of any body weight or body shape! We've helped more than 400,000 people lose their weight and have a healthier lifestyle. Hope this book will also help you!

Have you ever failed losing weight many times? Do you still have the courage to try again and want to kick out your overweight? Do you want to be more healthier, less illness, be more beautiful, and still can be able to have delicious foods?

Do you often have no enough time to cook foods? Do you want to just put all the ingredients into the instant pot and then wait for it to finish the cooking process, and you can have a very delicious foods in a few minutes? Keep reading, you will find all the answers by following this book!

You can follow the keto lifestyle with an Instant Pot to prepare quick, healthy, and delicious meals that improve your overall health. The ketogenic diet emphasizes a low carb, high fat, and adequate protein meal plan. When you are following the keto diet, you will eat low carb and high-fat foods. Following this diet, your body will enter into a state of ketosis. When in ketosis, your liver produces ketones to fuel your brain and muscles, instead of glucose. Normally, if you use carbs as your fuel source, you can gain weight and be deprived of energy. Luckily for you, this book offers a quick and easy guide on using the instant pot and keto diet.

By following a ketogenic diet, you will get too many benefits, below are the some them:

No starvation.

Lose your weight faster.

Have a stable energy level.

Enjoy **increased endurance.**

Get rid of your insulin resistance.

Improve your blood profile indicators.

Reduce or eliminate your diabetic medications.

Regulate your blood pressure without medication.

Be more smarter by increasing your mental focus and clearing your mental fog.

The recipes you will make using your instant pot are low in carbohydrates and can reduce your weight. With a total of **101 recipes**, you are certain to have a new meal to try out every day for the next couple of months. You will also learn everything needed to know about the Instant Pot and keto diet, such as:

1. **Everything About the Instant Pot?**
2. Brief Overview of the Ketogenic Diet?
3. **Benefits of the Ketogenic Diet?**
4. How Does the Instant Pot work?
5. **Many many Useful advice and more!**
6. 14- Day Meal Plan

Finally, this book will open the grand world of tasty foods to you. All the recipes you find in this book are unique, delicious, easy to make, and with ingredients that are inexpensive at your grocery store. At the end of the book, you will also find a 14-day meal plan, which will provide you a great start for your ketogenic journey. Consider this cookbook not just your average cookbook but as your best friend. This book should be used daily, as it contains a multitude of healthy and amazing recipes you can enjoy each day.

We have made this book very easy to follow. We have put all of what we have known and experienced about ketogenic diet into this book. You will get the tips and essential knowledge of the ketogenic diet and Instant Pot spending just a few minutes reading. This book is not just a good guide for your ketogenic diet, and it's not just for losing weight; we believe it will be your lifelong companion. You will find amazing results in the next few weeks when you stand before the mirror.

Happy reading!

Chapter 1: Everything About the Ketogenic Diet

There are many low-carb diets available. One of the most popular is the "ketogenic diet". More and more people are turning to the ketogenic diet because of the various advantages this diet carries. The ketogenic diet is a powerful way to lose weight and offers multiple benefits to leading a healthy eating lifestyle that fad diets do not. In this chapter, you will learn everything you need to know about ketogenic diet.

What is the Ketogenic Diet?

The ketogenic diet is a high-fat, moderate protein, low-carbohydrate diet. This diet concentrates on decreasing your carbohydrate intake and replacing it with healthy fats and proteins. Normally, your body burns carbohydrates to convert into glucose, which is then carried around your body and is essential for brain fuel. However, when your body has low amounts of carbohydrates, the liver will convert fat into fatty acids and ketone bodies. The ketone bodies then move into the brain and replace glucose as the primary energy source.

The ketogenic diet was created for you to reach a state of ketosis. Ketosis is a metabolic state where your body produces ketones. Ketones are produced by your liver and are used as fuel towards your body and brain instead of glucose. To make ketones, you must consume a substantial number of carbs and bare minimum amount of proteins. The traditional ketogenic diet contains a 4:1 ratio by weight of fat to combined protein and carbohydrate. This is accomplished by eliminating high-carbohydrate foods, such as starchy fruits, vegetables, breads, grains, pasta, and sugar while boosting the consumption of foods high in fats, such as nuts, cream, and butter. The bottom line is the ketogenic diet is a low-carb diet useful in burning body fat.

Benefits of the Ketogenic Diet.

The ketogenic diet comes with many positive benefits. For beginners, it has been used to treat epileptic seizures and various other diseases, including cancers and Alzheimer's. Overall, the ketogenic diet can be used to improve and enhance your health by preventing and controlling the substances in your body. Here are some of the benefits you can enjoy through ketogenic diet:

1. Weight Loss.

The ketogenic diet focuses on keeping carbs to a minimum. Studies have proven that ketogenic practitioners lose weight easier and faster, compared to other people. Why? Because on a ketogenic diet, you will drastically reduce the number of carbohydrates in each meal.

When you begin to consume fewer carbohydrates, the excess water in your body will shed. Thereby, reducing the levels of insulin in your body, which would directly impact your sodium levels, cultivating weight loss.

2. Diminishes Your Appetite.

Following a low-carb diet can alleviate your hunger. The worst side effects of this diet is feeling hungry. Hunger is the main reason why many people bail. However, when you follow the low-carb diet, your appetite will be reduced. The more you cut carbs from your diet, the more you add protein and healthy fats. Thus, the fewer calories you consume. In other words, once you eliminate carbohydrates from your diet, your appetite will decrease and you end up consuming fewer calories, without even trying to eat less.

3. Decrease in Blood Pressure.

When your blood pressure is high or if you suffer from hypertension, you become prone to developing several health issues, like heart disease, kidney failure, or stroke. One of the most efficient ways to reduce your blood pressure is to follow a low-carb diet. Successfully following a low-carb diet, your exposure to diseases will be reduced. Research has also shown that reducing your consumption of carbohydrates leads to a significant reduction in blood pressure, thus reducing your risk of developing various diseases.

4. Improves Your HDL Cholesterol.

HDL cholesterol is a special kind of protein that runs by transferring the "bad cholesterol" from your body and into your liver, where the cholesterol is either exerted or reused. When your HDL cholesterol level is high, your cholesterol deposits within your blood vessel walls, and this helps to prevent blockage that can provoke heart disease or heart pain. High-fat diets like the ketogenic diet are known for raising your blood vessels with HDL, which means you can reduce the risk of developing cardiovascular disease.

5. Improves Digestion.

The ketogenic diet contains low carbs, low grains, and low sugars, which can drastically improve your digestion. When you consume carbs and sugars on a regular basis, it can result in gas, bloating, stomach pains, and constipation. Reducing sugars and carbohydrates in your diet can renew your digestive system.

6. Reduces Triglycerides.

Triglycerides are also known as fat molecules. Increased levels of triglycerides have been connected to heart health. Thus, it is important to lower triglyceride levels, which can be done through the ketogenic diet. The more carbohydrates you consume, the more triglycerides you will have in your blood, which can provoke heart disease. When you cut down carbohydrate consumption, the number of triglycerides in the body will be dramatically reduced.

7. Increases Energy.

A ketogenic diet can increase your energy levels in multiple ways. It increases your mitochondrial function, and at the same time decreases the harmful radicals inside your body. Making you feel more energetic and restored.

8. Improves Mental Health.

The ketone bodies released when following ketogenic diet have been directly connected to mental health. Research have shown that increased ketone levels can lead to stabilization of neurotransmitters, like dopamine and serotonin. This stabilization can help to fight mood swings, depression, and other psychological issues.

Why the Ketogenic Diet Can Lose Weight Faster than Other Diets

Obesity has become one of the largest health epidemics in the world. Many have tried multiple methods to fight obesity and excess weight, but their methods were not successful. To overcome obesity and lose weight, you must change your diet. The ketogenic diet has worked for many to preserve muscle mass and shed excess fat, without putting much effort.

The sole purpose of the ketogenic diet is to make your body enter a state of glycogen deprivation and maintain a state of ketosis, which is great for weight-loss. Usually, in carb-based diets, carbohydrates are converted into glucose, which is then used as the main fuel source for the body and brain. The remaining glucose is then converted to glycogen and stored in your liver for later use. When your glycogen steers are full, the excess is stored as fat, thus leading to weight gain.

This means that the main cause of weight gain is not eating fats, but the excessive consumption of carbs. Once you eliminate or reduce your carb intake and increase your fat intake, your body changes from burning carbs for energy to burning fats for energy. This means that the excess fats stored in your body will be burnt for your energy source, thus leading to weight loss.

As well with this, the ketogenic lifestyle can also help suppress your appetite. This is largely because the foods you eat under the ketogenic diet, like fats and protein are quite filling; thus, you will stay full longer and don't feel the urge to eat often.

What Happens to Your Body Under the Ketogenic Diet?

The reason the ketogenic diet is so efficient when it comes to improving your health, losing weight, lowering health risks, gaining more energy, and mental clarity is because of ketosis, which is a status when your body produces ketones to provide energy for your brain and body. Usually, your body will break down carbohydrates and turn them into glucose for a source of fuel. But when you adjust to a ketogenic diet, your body will go from storing carbohydrates to burning fat.

Over time when you have successfully entered ketosis, your body will adapt to this new eating regime. During this short period of transitioning to ketogenic lifestyle, you may experience side effects.

Here is what may happen when your body enters the ketogenic diet:

1. Ketogenic Flu.

In the first week of starting the ketogenic diet, it could be challenging for some. Your body might be used to relying mainly on glucose for energy, so it will need to transition to use ketones for fuel. You may begin to feel tired, unmotivated, and lethargic; this is generally caused because of salt deficiency and dehydration that is promoted by the temporary increase in urinating. It also implies that your body will need to take more time to adjust to the new ingredients being digested and the ingredients it is not accustomed to consuming.

Some of symptoms you may experience with Keto flu:

- Brain fogginess.
- Nausea.
- Cravings.
- Irritability.
- Sniffles.
- Coughing.
- Heart palpitations.
- Dizziness.
- Insomnia.

To help cope with the ketogenic flu, you should increase your water and salt intake, as this can prevent you from feeling lousy and tired.

2. Temporary Fatigue.

Feeling fatigued and weak is one of the most common side effects in entering ketosis for most dieters. This is mostly because your body is being deprived of carbohydrates, which is the only fuel source that your body has been used to. After a week or two, when your body has successfully adapted to burning fats, you will feel more energized and sense an improvement in mental clarity.

In the meantime, how can you cope with temporary fatigue? One thing you can do is take vitamin supplements. One essential nutrient your body always needs is Vitamin B5. If you do not have Vitamin B5, you will start to feel more fatigued or lethargic.

Vitamin B5 helps the adrenaline by boosting metabolism with more energy. Go to the health store and purchase Vitamin B5, as it can help with temporary fatigue during your ketogenic journey.

3. Bad Breath.

Something you should expect from your body under the ketogenic diet is stinky breath. It's not because the foods you are eating is causing bad breath.

Bad breath is a common sign of ketosis because of the elevated levels of ketones in your blood. Notably, it's caused by a specific ketone known as acetone. This type of ketone usually leaves your body through your breath and urine, thus creating stinky breath.

Luckily for you, this symptom will last a short amount of time. As with fatigue, bad breath will go away once your body is fully adapted to the ketogenic diet. And while waiting for your body to adjust to this diet, you can brush your teeth more frequently and use mouthwash more often.

4. Leg Cramps.

Under the ketogenic diet, you may experience muscle cramps. These muscle cramps are common because of hyponatremia, which happens when your level of sodium in the blood is low. To cope with muscle cramps, you can add an extra teaspoon of salt in your meals and be well hydrated.

5. Headaches.

As with many changes in your diet, headaches can occur for no reason. It is possibly you may become light-headed and start to have flu-like symptoms, which could occur over a few days. These headaches normally happen because of a mineral imbalance due to diet change. One way to resolve this is to add one-quarter teaspoon of salt to a glass of water and drink it. If you are just beginning the keto lifestyle, you should increase both your salt and water intake for the first couple of days to combat this effectively.

6. Difficulty Sleeping.

Another symptom of embarking on the ketogenic diet is trouble sleeping. Many newbies to this diet often find themselves staying up late at night, or frequently wake up at night after cutting down on carbs. Remember, this is all temporary. Over time, you will not have trouble sleeping. In fact, many people who remained on the ketogenic diet had their quality of sleep improved significantly.

7. Constipation.

In your first week of the ketogenic diet, you may experience constipation because your body may need time to adjust to this new eating regime. To help you cope with this symptom, you can eat more vegetables loaded with fiber. This will keep your intestines moving and increase bowel movements. You can also drink more water to help fight dehydration, which is the contributing factor for constipation.

These are the most common signs of what your body could go through when embark on ketogenic diet. Not everyone experiences the same symptoms or may encounter different symptoms. Do not feel discouraged or unmotivated about the diet. Remember, within a few weeks the symptoms will pass and you can reap the positive benefits from ketogenic lifestyle.

Dos and Don'ts of Ketogenic Diet

If you are not familiar with the Keto, there are some mistakes you could make that can keep you back from having good health and the benefits of this diet. To enhance the success with the ketogenic diet, here are some dos and don'ts about following the diet:

1. Don't increase your carb intake.

The ketogenic diet is a low-carb diet, which means you should lower your carb intake. There is not a specific number of carbs you should have in a diet. A lot of people follow a diet in which they consume 100 to 150 grams of carbs a day. To achieve ketosis, you must make sure your carbohydrate intake is low.

You may find a balanced number of carbs to consume, but most keto dieters manage the state of ketosis by consuming between 20 to 100 grams of carbs a day.

2. Don't fear fat.

If you are on a ketogenic diet, don't be scared of fat. Especially if you consume healthy fats like Omega-3s, monounsaturated fats, and saturated fats. This is encouraged in the ketogenic diet plan; it is better to set a 60 to 70% fat intake as a limit. To achieve these levels of fat, you must consume meat and healthy fats, such as olive oil, lard, butter, and coconut or alternatives on a daily basis.

3. Don't eat fast food.

If you are busy and don't have time to cook, you may turn to fast foods. However, don't even think about it. Fast foods are incredibly unhealthy and can deter you from your keto journey. Fast foods contain too many harmful chemicals and preservatives, and some fast foods don't use real cheese, and meats that contain hidden sugars among the ingredients.

4. Do increase your protein intake.

Protein is an essential and important nutrient which is needed for your body. It can soothe your appetite and burn fat more than any other nutrient. If you look in general ways, protein is said to be very effective in weight loss, increase muscle mass, and improve your body composition.

5. Do increase your sodium intake.

When you reduce your carbohydrate consumption, your insulin levels fall, which in turn gets rid of extra sodium stored in your body, causing problems such as sodium deficiency. If your body experiences sodium deficiency, you will experience exhaustion, headaches, constipations, etc.

To get rid of this problem, you must increase your sodium intake on a keto diet. You can just add a teaspoon of salt to daily meals or drink a glass of water with a ¼ teaspoon of salt mixed with it.

6. Do be patient.

It is common nature for us to seek immediate gratification. When you start a diet, you may be discouraged to continue if you are not experiencing the benefits immediately. Losing weight and being healthy takes time. Your body needs to allow itself time to start burning fat instead of glucose in order to do this. It may take a couple days or a couple weeks, but be patient and don't bail on the diet.

Important Tips for Successful Ketogenic Journey

If you are just beginning the ketogenic journey, it may be hard for you to stick to this new eating regime, even if you know it's good for you. We are regularly influenced by unhealthy foods around us, and the accessibility of these foods make them hard to pass up. Changing your diet is a long-term process, not something you do right off the bat. Here are some valuable tips for a successful ketogenic journey:

1. Gradually follow the ketogenic diet.

A common mistake that many do when starting the ketogenic diet is immediately eliminating carbohydrates. Doing this is not healthy for your body. While this may work in the short term, doing this can cause serious health problems over the long-term.

Give yourself time to maneuver into the keto lifestyle by making small but essential changes, like giving up one carb source every week or so. It's critical to give your body time to adjust to changes. An excellent way to overcome transition discomfort is to add a healthy nutrient source to your diet each time you take something unhealthy out. For example, if you use all-purpose flour, start substituting it with almond flour or coconut flour.

2. Drink lots of water.

When you start the ketogenic diet, your body will have a difficult time keeping the proper amount of water you need, so staying perfectly hydrated is the best way to go about it. Drink eight, 8-ounce glasses, which is equivalent to 2 liters every day. To know if you are well-hydrated is to determine the color of your urine. Whenever your urine is light yellow or clear, you are properly hydrated.

3. Turn your favorite foods into ketogenic foods.

Thinking of the foods you are not allowed to eat can become quite discouraging. Instead, learn keto-friendly versions of your favorite dishes. There's plenty of ketogenic cookbooks and internet recipes for tips and ideas on how to turn your favorite dishes into tasty ketogenic friendly versions.

Following the ketogenic diet does not mean depriving yourself from your favorite meals, but about improving your diet and making it healthier. As the keto-diet is high in fat, you will maintain all the flavors and texture from your favorite recipes. In many cases, the ketogenic diet has enhanced the flavor in many recipes.

4. Don't be afraid to ask for advice.

If you have any questions or confusions about the ketogenic diet, don't be afraid to ask for help. Ask professionals, ketogenic dieters, and maybe even certified nutritionists for advice, recipes, and experiences. You will be surprised by other people's experiences and some of the information they have to share.

6. Be aware of alcohol consumption.

You can still drink alcohol while on the keto diet without ruining the process. This is one of the great aspects of this diet. However, don't go overboard and drink all the time. It is preferred to go for unsweetened liquors, like scotch, tequila, vodka, whiskey, rum, and reduced-carb beer.

7. Be mindful of condiments and sauces.

Not all condiments and sauces are healthy or ketogenic friendly. If you must use sauce and condiments, choose ones that are low in carbs, like soy sauce, lemon, salad dressings, mayonnaise, mustard, olive oil, and coconut oil (just to name a few).

In cases in which you can't tell if something is keto-friendly or not, you can always ask the server or chef. If they can't tell as well, it would be best to not use the sauce.

8. Be patient.

Even though the ketogenic lifestyle is known for rapid weight loss, losing weight will take some time. Don't quit the diet when you are not experiencing quick results. Getting rid of fat will change throughout the day. Don't get too worked up with a scale, instead be patient and trust that the ketogenic diet will help you lose weight.

9. Use vitamins and mineral salts.

Foods high in carbohydrates contain many micronutrients, such as vitamins and minerals. When you stop eating carbohydrates, it can cause nutritional deficiency to your body. To help fight through this, you should use proper vitamins that can provide your body with nutrients.

10. Restock your fridge and pantry.

If you are preparing to follow the ketogenic diet, the best way to begin is to get rid of unfriendly keto ingredients from your kitchen and restock with keto-friendly ingredients. This will help you become more attentive and help you resist the urge to eat unfriendly keto recipes.

Get everything you need to prepare your meals and plan ahead to avoid any inconveniences that may make you lose track of your diet.

What Foods Should Be on Your Plate?

There are specific guidelines for you to follow on the ketogenic diet. It has been designed to help people with various diseases and for those looking to shed extra weight. It will be best to take note of all the healthy and essential foods that are allowed on this diet.

Below is a list of healthy ingredients you should include on your menu:

Vegetables

You will eat tons of vegetables on the keto diet. However, you should be more attentive about the kinds of vegetables you consume. Eat vegetables high in nutrients and low in carbohydrates. It also will be good if you go for organic vegetables, as they contain fewer chemicals and pesticides. The best advantage you have for eating non-starchy vegetables is that they do not raise your blood glucose levels, which would throw your ketosis off balance. Non-starchy vegetables can also help you lose weight by reducing your appetite because they are loaded with fiber.

Here is a short list of some of the best vegetables to eat on the ketogenic diet:

Lettuce

Lettuce is the best vegetable for a ketogenic lifestyle. Lettuce contains few carbohydrates and is a great source of potassium, protein, fiber, and energy. Lettuce also contains many beneficial minerals and vitamins including iron, magnesium, calcium, phosphorus, sodium, niacin, folate, vitamin B6, vitamin A, and vitamin K. Lettuce can also be a healthy ketogenic alternative for hamburger buns and taco shells.

Broccoli

Broccoli is healthy and delicious and also rich in nutrients, fiber, calcium, protein, and potassium.

Spinach

Spinach is one of the best vegetables rich in potassium, proteins, and iron. Spinach is also delicious and can be used for salads, stuffing, side dishes, and much more.

Cauliflower

Cauliflower is an excellent source of choline, dietary fiber, omega-3 fatty acids, phosphorus, biotin, vitamins B1, B2, and B3. You can use cauliflower to prepare rice, pizza crusts, hummus, and breadsticks.

Tomatoes

Tomatoes carry many positive health benefits and are a great source of vitamin A, C, and K. Including these vitamins, tomatoes are high in potassium, which can reduce blood pressure levels and decrease stroke risks. When you roast tomatoes with olive oil, you can enhance the lycopene content, boosting its effects. It can also protect heart health and reduce the risk of cancer.

Avocados

Avocados are rich in omega oils. Avocados can be eaten in a combination of salads or mixed with other ingredients such as yogurt and nuts. They are high in potassium and fiber and is great for your metabolism and heart. Most grocery stores will sell them in semi-ripened condition, so you can keep them for up to a week as they ripen. Avocados also have high oil content and minerals, which allow it to reduce your appetite and provide nutrients all around for your body.

Asparagus

Asparagus is a great source of minerals and vitamins, including vitamin A, C, and K. Studies have also shown that asparagus can help cope with anxiety and protect mental health. Consider eating roasted asparagus for dinner or add raw asparagus in your salads.

Mushrooms

Mushrooms contain strong anti-inflammatory properties, which can improve inflammation for those who have metabolic problems. Mushrooms are also packed with copper, potassium, protein, and selenium. It is also a great source of phosphorus, niacin, pantothenic acid, and zinc, especially if you cook them until brown.

Zucchini

Zucchini is low-carb vegetable and a great source of vitamin A, magnesium, potassium, copper, phosphorus, and folate. Zucchini is also high in omega-3 fatty acids, protein, zinc, and niacin. If you include zucchini in your diet, it can lead to an optimal healthy lifestyle.

Bell Peppers

Bell peppers are nutritious and packed with fiber and vitamins. Bell peppers also contain anti-inflammatory properties that can be useful on the ketogenic diet.

Proteins

Following a ketogenic diet requires you to find a source of protein. Proteins consist of amino acids, which are essential nutrients for your body and brain. You must consume protein, as it is your primary fuel source on this diet. Here are some things you might consider adding to your plate:

Meat and Poultry

Any kind of meat can be used for the ketogenic diet, especially given they are high in fat. Always choose meat from grass-fed and wild animal sources. Avoid hot dogs and sausages, and meat covered with starch or processed sauces.

Fish

Fish is another great source of protein. As with meat and poultry, always choose organic and wild fish that are caught naturally. Such examples of good fish include salmon, trout, tuna, shrimp, cod, lobster, and catfish.

Eggs

Eggs are an incredible source of protein and contain low-carbs, especially the egg yolk.

Fats and Oils

Since you will need to burn fat for energy, you must assure to include fats and oils in your diet. Instead of vegetable oil, go for olive oil, coconut oil, avocado oil, and ghee.

You should also buy oils that are rich in polyunsaturated fats and have a low smoke level; these oils will retain their fatty acids. Such oils include walnut oil, flax oil, hemp seed oil, and grapeseed oil.

Dairy Products

For a ketogenic diet, consider consuming raw and organic dairy products. You can use cheeses and creams to prepare ketogenic meals. Examples of the best dairy products to include in your diet are mozzarella cheese, cheddar cheese, parmesan cheese, cottage cheese, sour cream, cream cheese, heavy whipping cream, and Greek yogurt.

Nuts and Seeds

Nuts have healthy fats and nutrients such as vitamin E. When you are choosing nuts, try to purchase roasted nuts because they will already have their anti-nutrients discarded. Best nuts and seeds for this diet include walnuts, almonds, and macadamias. They are low in calories and can help you control your carbohydrate count. You can also use products such as almond flour as an alternative to regular flour.

Fruits

You can eat fruits on the keto diet but keep in moderation. Some fruits retract you from reaching ketosis. Berries though, are the most advantageous as they are packed with nutrition and hold a low level in sugar.

What Foods Shouldn't Be on Your Plate?

For you to successfully reach ketosis, you must do your best to prevent and rid your body of foods that will hold you back from your goal. Most foods you should avoid are high in carbohydrates and do not allow your body to burn fat for energy. Here is a general list of the types of foods to avoid:

Ground Vegetables

Vegetables that are grown and picked from the ground are high in carbohydrates and can take you away from ketosis. Such vegetables include potatoes, beets, radishes, carrots, onions, and parsnips.

Fruits

You should avoid most fruits while following the ketogenic diet. Fruits contain fructose (similar to glucose), and is bad for reaching ketosis. Not only should you avoid fruits, but avoid products made with fresh fruit, such as juices and extracts. If you do eat fruits, keep it in moderation.

Grains

Obviously, you should avoid foods that are made with processed grains. Grains contain additives that can negatively affect your insulin levels. Such grains include bread, pasta, cakes, breadcrumbs, cookies, and pastries.

Diet Soda

Diet soda claims to not contain sugars or carbs; it contains artificial sweeteners which are equally as detrimental as regular sugar. Artificial sweeteners can enhance your carbohydrate intake and prevent you from reaching the metabolic state of ketosis.

Alcohol

Most alcohol beverages consist of no, or low carbs, but can still be bad for a keto lifestyle. Alcohol can prevent the fat burning process or slow it down dramatically, because your body will need to burn away the alcohol first before the fat. If you want to be successful with this diet, limit your alcohol intake.

Processed Foods

You should avoid processed or packaged foods. Such foods are stuffed with artificial additives that can stray you away from ketosis. Instead of choosing the processed foods, pick organic and real ingredients.

This is all you need to know about the ketogenic diet. Some people and sources will tell you different, but you get the concept. The ketogenic diet and instant pot have plenty in common. It can be used together make fast, tasty, and healthy dishes that will improve your life. Since the keto diet asks you to avoid greasy foods, the instant pot helps by softening up foods using pressure and heat. With all this said, let's use the instant pot to prepare ketogenic meals for better health.

Chapter 2: Everything About the Instant Pot

The Instant Pot is a revolutionary multi-cooker that can cook foods in a matter of minutes. The pressure cooker uses both pressure and heat to cook your foods through. The multi-cooker also retains the nutrients from your pressure-cooked meals, because the pressure cooker steams food quickly and evenly. In this chapter, you will learn everything about the Instant Pot and learn how to use it like a professional.

What is an Instant Pot AND It's Benefits?

The Instant Pot is a multi-cooker which was designed to prepare a variety of meals quickly and deliciously. With an Instant Pot, you can pressure cook, slow cook, sauté, make yogurt, make rice, and more, and this can all be done by pressing a couple of buttons and letting the machine do the rest. Most modules also come with an automatic shut-off button, so that your food will not overcook once ready. The instant pot also has plenty of benefits, including:

The instant pot cooks foods faster.
An instant pot uses pressure and heat to cook; it will take a much shorter time to cook foods through completely. For example, if you use an oven to cook chicken, it may take an hour. But, with an Instant Pot, you may only need 20 minutes or possibly less to do the same job.

The instant pot retains vitamins and minerals.
Pressure cooking allows you to retain more vitamins and minerals through pressure cooking vegetables, as opposed to boiling and steaming. The longer you cook, the more nutrition that is lost from your food, in particular for

vegetables. Since the Instant Pot takes a matter of minutes to cook, it will retain most of its vitamins and minerals needed to fuel your body.

As well with this, pressure cooking can make foods easier to digest, such as beans and lentils. You can cook foods in the Instant Pot without worrying about upsetting your stomach.

The instant pot is easy to use.
When you cook on the stovetop or in the oven, you need your full attention to make sure you don't ruin the meal. The Instant Pot is easy to use; you just place the ingredients in and allow the machine to do the rest.

The instant pot doesn't need anything else.
An Instant Pot is the only kitchen appliance you need. You can cook breakfast, lunch, dinner, and dessert, all with the Instant Pot. And in this book, you will learn an abundant amount of ketogenic instant pot recipes.

Including this, the Instant Pot is also easy to clean. All you do is remove the gasket from the cover and wash it with warm water.

How Does the Instant Pot Work?

The Instant Pot is a fast way to cook delicious meals through pressure cooking. Pressure-cooking is a cooking method that uses steam sealed in a pressure cooker, it is an airtight cooking pot. If you add water, the pressure will trap the vapor that rises from the liquid. This will then raise the pressure inside the pressure cooker, along with the temperature of the water. With the increased in temperature and pressure, the cooking process speeds up.

It's easy to use an Instant Pot: All you need to do is adding your ingredients to the pot and adjust the settings. When learning how to use an Instant Pot, you must be aware of what these buttons are and what they do:

Instant Pot Control Panel.

Here we will explain in detail about the different controls and sets on the Instant Pot:

Manual: This is your main button. All you need to do is press the button and manually set the pressure and cooking time.

Sauté: This button allows you to sauté and brown foods. When using this button, you will cook with the lid off (enabling you to stir your ingredients). You can adjust the heat from sauté by pressing the normal setting, more, or less. Normal is for regular browning, more is for stir-frying, and less is for simmering (such as thickening sauces).

Keep Warm/Cancel: This button cancels any function and turns your Instant Pot off. If your cooking is done, the Instant Pot will automatically enter a *keep warm* mode and stay there for up to 10 hours. You cancel the function at any time.

Timer: This button is for delayed cooking. You first need to select a cooking function and make any required adjustments. You can then adjust the timer button using the +/- buttons.

Slow Cook: Pressing this button turns your Instant Pot into a slow-cooker.

Pressure: When you cook in manual button, this button will adjust your pressure to low, medium, or high.

Yogurt: Pressing this button allows your Instant Pot to make yogurt.

Soup: This button automatically sets your Instant Pot to high pressure for 30 minutes. You can adjust the settings to select a shorter or longer cooking time.

Meat/Stew: This button automatically sets your Instant Pot to high pressure for 35 minutes.

Bean/Chili: This button automatically sets your Instant Pot to high pressure for 30 minutes.

Poultry: This button automatically sets your Instant Pot to high pressure for 15 minutes.

Rice: This button automatically sets your Instant Pot to low pressure and cooks rice based on the amount of water in the pot.

Multi-Grain: This button automatically sets your Instant Pot to high pressure for 40 minutes.

Porridge: This button automatically sets your Instant Pot to high pressure for 20 minutes.

Steam: This button automatically sets your Instant Pot to high for 10 minutes.

When you use a pressure cooker, you must know how to release pressure. You can do it two ways with the Instant Pot; either through natural release or quick release. The natural release allows pressure to release on its own naturally. The quick release is when you turn the valve on the top from the 'sealing' setting to the 'venting' setting.

How to Choose a Good Instant Pot

There are various versions of the Instant Pot available in the market. But which is the best one for you? From the most popular 6-quart version to larger and more advanced varieties. Here are some options to consider when choosing an Instant Pot:

IP-DUO60.
This is the most popular model of the Instant Pot. It is a 7-in-1 multifunctional countertop appliance; which combines a pressure cooker, slow cooker, rice cooker, yogurt maker, steamer, warmer, and sauté/browning functionality.

IP-DUO Plus60.
The Plus 60 is an upgrade to the regular IP-DUO60. This includes more settings, such as the *Cake, Egg,* and *Sterilize* buttons. The alarm clock on

this Instant Pot is a blue LCD screen. The Instant Pot's inner bowl also has more comprehensive max/min fill lines.

IP-DUO50.

This Instant Pot holds 5-quarts.

IP-DUO80.

This Instant Pot has a capacity of 8-quarts. It is pricier than the others, but the extra space might be useful.

IP-LUX60 V3.

This Instant Pot has cake and egg cook settings in the control panel. However, this Instant Pot does not have the Beans/Chili, Poultry, or Yogurt setting, nor an option to cook on low pressure. It also arrives without some of the accessories seen on other models.

IP-Smart Bluetooth.

This Instant Pot is a 6-quart with all the basic functions, and can connect via Bluetooth to your phone; so you can program and monitor cooking from anywhere using the Instant Pot Smart Cooker app.

Choosing a good Instant Pot should not be complicated. It is also best to purchase a new appliance and not used, as they may have broken buttons and complications along with it.

Dos and Don'ts of Instant Pot

If you are just starting out using an Instant Pot, it will be helpful for you to learn what you should do and not do when using the Instant Pot. Here are some valuable tips for cooking with an Instant Pot:

Don't add ingredients to the Instant Pot without the Inner Pot.

It would be a pain if you were to pour ingredients into your Instant Pot without the Inner Pot. Believe me; this happens a lot. Doing this will cause damage and be time-consuming to clean.

Don't press the timer button to set the cooking time.

People often mistake the 'timer' button for setting the cook time, and then wonder why the Instant Pot isn't working. Always make sure the 'timer' button is not lit before you leave.

Don't overfill your instant pot.

New users frequently fill their Instant Pot with too much food and liquid, which risks clogging the venting knob. To ensure you never overfill, ascertain you never go past the max line indicated on the inner pot.

Don't use quick release for foamy foods or when your Instant Pot is overfilled.

Many new users are confused when it comes to Quick Pressure Release and Natural Pressure Release. If you use Quick Release when cooking foamy foods, such as grains, beans, or applesauce, it could splatter everywhere. To prevent this from happening, use natural release or release the pressure gradually.

Do pay attention to cooking times.

While cooking times for a recipe is a great indicator of the amount of time it should take for your food to cook, the actual cooking time can vary. This is because different ingredients are used and done in different situations. For example, various meats will take different times to soften up. To make sure your foods are cooked through, do not rush through the recipe and be mindful of the end result. Test a small piece from the recipe to ascertain it is cooked through before completely removing from your Instant Pot.

Do read all the instructions very carefully.

When you purchase your Instant Pot, read all the instructions carefully to prevent any damages, mishaps, and to make sure nobody gets hurt.

Do inspect your Instant Pot carefully.

It is important you keep your instant pot extremely clean so that it remains a reliable appliance and in working condition. If parts on your pressure cooker begin to wear out, they should be replaced by original parts, or you risk permanently damaging the appliance.

Do clean your Instant Pot.

As I said earlier, you must always clean and take care of your Instant Pot to ensure it is in optimal condition. After cooking with your Instant Pot, remove the inner pot and wash it with warm water and soap. Then, use a dish rag to wipe the outer parts of the pressure cooker.

Chapter 3: Delicious Soups, Stews, and Chilies

1. Classy Creamy Mushroom Stew

Time: 40 minutes

Servings: 6

Ingredients:

- 1 pound cremini mushrooms, sliced
- 1 celery stalk, chopped
- 2 Tablespoons green onions, chopped
- 2 garlic cloves, minced
- 2 cups beef stock
- ½ cup heavy cream
- 5 ounces cream cheese, softened
- 1 Tablespoon unsalted butter, melted
- 1 Tablespoon lemon juice
- 1 teaspoon fresh or dried thyme
- 2 Tablespoons fresh sage, chopped
- 1 bay leaf
- 1 teaspoon salt
- 1 teaspoon fresh ground black pepper

Instructions:

1. Rinse the mushrooms, pat dry.
2. Press Sauté button on Instant Pot. Melt the butter.
3. Add green onions, garlic. Cook for 1 minute.
4. Add mushrooms, celery, and garlic. Sauté until vegetables are softened.
5. Press Keep Warm/Cancel setting to stop Sauté mode.
6. Add remaining ingredients. Stir well.
7. Close and seal lid. Select Meat/Stew button. Set cooking time to 20 minutes.

8. Once done, Instant Pot will switch to Keep Warm mode.
9. Remain on Keep Warm for 10 minutes.
10. When done, use Quick Release setting; turn valve from sealing to venting to release pressure quickly. Open lid carefully. Stir ingredients.
11. Serve. Garnish with green onion, grated parmesan cheese.

2. Divine Cabbage Beef Soup

Time: 40 minutes

Servings: 6

Ingredients:

- 1 pound lean ground beef
- 1 head green cabbage, chopped
- 1 head red cabbage, chopped
- 1 celery stalk, chopped
- 1 can (28-ounce) diced tomatoes
- 3 cups water
- 1 teaspoon salt
- 1 teaspoon fresh ground black pepper
- 1 Tablespoon fresh parsley, chopped

Instructions:

1. Press Sauté button on Instant Pot.
2. Add ground beef. Sauté until no longer pink; drain.
3. Press Keep Warm/Cancel setting to stop Sauté mode.
4. Return ground beef to Instant Pot. Add cabbage, celery, diced tomatoes, water, parsley, salt, and pepper. Stir well.
5. Close and seal lid. Press Meat/Stew. Cook on High Pressure for 20 minutes.
6. Once done, Instant Pot will switch to Keep Warm mode.
7. Remain in Keep Warm mode for 10 minutes.

8. When done, use Quick-Release. Open lid carefully. Stir ingredients.
9. Serve. Garnish with fresh parsley.

3. Creamy Garlic Chicken Noodle Soup

Time: 40 minutes

Servings: 4

Ingredients:

- 1 pound chicken breasts, boneless, skinless
- 1 pound spiralized squash noodles (or any keto-friendly alternative)
- 1 celery stalk, chopped
- 1 cup carrots, chopped
- 2 green onions, chopped
- 6 cups chicken broth
- 2 Tablespoons coconut oil
- 1 teaspoon salt (to taste)
- 1 teaspoon fresh ground black pepper)

Instructions:

1. Rinse the chicken, pat dry.
2. Press the Sauté button on your Instant Pot. Heat the coconut oil.
3. Add chicken breasts. Sauté until brown on both sides, and cooked through.
4. Remove chicken and shred with a fork.
5. Add celery, carrots, and green onion to Instant Pot. Sauté for 3 minutes.
6. Press Keep Warm/Cancel setting to stop Sauté mode.
7. Return shredded chicken and remaining ingredients to Instant Pot. Stir well.
8. Close and seal lid. Press Soup button. Cook for 30 minutes.
9. When done, set to quick pressure release to vent steam. Open lid carefully. Stir.

10.   Spoon into serving bowls. Garnish with fresh green onions.

4. Amazing Spinach, Kale, and Artichoke Soup

Time: 25 minutes

Servings: 4

Ingredients:

- 1 bunch of kale, stemmed and chopped
- 4 cups spinach
- 1-ounce jar artichoke hearts, drained and chopped
- 4 cups low-sodium chicken broth
- ¼ cup cheddar cheese, shredded
- ¼ cup mozzarella cheese, shredded
- 1 Tablespoon butter, melted
- 1 Tablespoon Italian seasoning
- 2 teaspoons fresh parsley, chopped
- 1 teaspoon salt
- 1 teaspoon fresh ground black pepper

Instructions:

1. Place all ingredients in Instant Pot. Stir well.
2. Close and seal lid. Press Manual setting. Cook for 15 minutes.
3. When done, use Quick-Release setting. Open lid carefully. Stir ingredients.
4. Serve.

5. Exquisite Chicken Avocado Soup

Time: 40 minutes

Servings: 4

Ingredients:

- 4 chicken breasts, boneless, skinless
- 1 tablespoon coconut oil
- 4 avocados, peeled and chopped
- 4 cups chicken broth
- Zest and juice from 1 lime
- 1 Tablespoon fresh cilantro, chopped
- 1 teaspoon salt
- 1 teaspoon fresh ground black pepper
- 2 tomatoes, chopped
- 2 garlic cloves, minced

Instructions:

1. Rinse the chicken, pat dry. Cut into strips.
2. Press Sauté button on Instant Pot. Melt the coconut oil.
3. Add chicken strips. Sauté until chicken no longer pink.
4. Add garlic and tomatoes. Stir well.
5. Press Keep Warm/Cancel setting to stop Sauté mode.
6. Add chopped avocados, chicken broth, lime juice, lime zest, cilantro, salt, and black pepper. Stir well.
7. Close and seal lid. Press Meat/Stew button on Instant Pot. Cook for 20 minutes.
8. Once done, Instant Pot will switch to Keep Warm mode.
9. Remain in Keep Warm mode for 10 minutes.
10. When done, use Quick-Release. Open lid carefully. Stir ingredients.
11. Serve.

6. Deluxe Cauliflower Stew

Time: 40 minutes

Servings: 4

Ingredients:

- 4 slices of bacon, cooked and crumbled
- 1 teaspoon coconut oil
- 1 head cauliflower, chopped into florets
- ¼ cup coconut flour
- 4 cups chicken broth
- 2 celery stalks, chopped
- 1 shallot, chopped
- 2 garlic cloves, minced
- 1 teaspoon salt
- 1 teaspoon fresh ground black pepper
- 1 Tablespoon fresh parsley, chopped

Instructions:

1. In a skillet or your Instant Pot, cook the bacon. Drain on paper towel. Set aside.
2. Press Sauté button on Instant Pot. Heat coconut oil.
3. Add cauliflower, celery, shallots, garlic cloves. Sauté until vegetables are softened.
4. Press Keep Warm/Cancel setting to stop Sauté mode.
5. Add coconut flour to ingredients. Stir well. Add chicken broth. Stir well.
6. Close and seal lid. Press Soup button. Cook 30 minutes.
7. When done, set to quick pressure release. Open lid carefully. Stir ingredients.
8. Serve. Garnish with fresh parsley.

7. Elegant Cauliflower and Cheddar Soup

Time: 50 minutes

Servings: 4

Ingredients:

- 2 Tablespoons butter
- 1 head cauliflower, chopped into florets
- 4 cups vegetable broth
- 1 red onion, diced
- 2 garlic cloves, minced
- ½ cup heavy cream
- ½ cup cheddar cheese, grated
- 1 teaspoon salt
- 1 teaspoon fresh ground black pepper

Instructions:

1. Press Sauté button on Instant Pot. Melt the butter.
2. Add red onion, garlic. Sweat for 1 minute.
3. Add cauliflower. Sauté until cauliflower is softened.
4. Press Keep Warm/Cancel setting to stop Sauté mode.
5. Add remaining ingredients. Mix well.
6. Close and seal lid. Press Soup button. Cook on high pressure for 30 minutes.
7. When done, Instant Pot will switch to Keep Warm mode.
8. Remain in Keep Warm mode for 10 minutes.
9. When done, use Quick-Release setting. Open lid carefully. Stir ingredients.
10. Serve.

8. Savory Beef and Squash Stew

Time: 50 minutes

Servings: 4

Ingredients:

- 1 pound lean ground beef
- 2 pounds butternut squash, peeled, chopped into chunks
- 1 (6-ounce) can sliced mushrooms
- 2 Tablespoons butter
- 4 cups beef broth
- 1 red onion, diced
- 2 garlic cloves, minced
- 1 teaspoon fresh rosemary, chopped
- 2 teaspoons paprika
- 1 teaspoon salt (to taste)
- 1 teaspoon fresh ground black pepper (to taste)

Instructions:

1. Press Sauté button on Instant Pot. Melt the butter.
2. Sauté the onions, garlic for 1 minute.
3. Add ground beef, butternut squash, and mushrooms.
4. Sauté until the ground beef is no longer pink and vegetables are softened.
5. Press Keep Warm/Cancel setting to stop Sauté mode.
6. Add beef stock, rosemary, paprika, salt, and black pepper. Mix well.
7. Close and seal lid. Press Soup button. Cook on high pressure for 30 minutes.
8. After 30 minutes, Instant Pot will switch to Keep Warm.
9. Remain in Keep Warm 10 minutes.
10. When done, use Quick-Release. Open lid carefully. Stir ingredients.
11. Serve.

9. Smoky Bacon Chili

Time: 40 minutes

Servings: 4

Ingredients:

- 8 slices bacon, cooked and crumbled
- 2 pounds lean ground beef
- 1 can (6-ounce) tomato paste
- 1 can (14-ounce) diced tomatoes
- 1 yellow onion, chopped
- 2 garlic cloves, minced
- 1 yellow bell pepper, chopped
- 1 red bell pepper, chopped
- 1 green bell pepper, chopped
- 2 Tablespoons fresh cilantro, chopped
- 1 Tablespoon smoked paprika
- 1 Tablespoon chili powder
- 2 teaspoons cumin
- 1 teaspoon salt (to taste)
- 1 teaspoon fresh ground black pepper (to taste)

Instructions:

1. Press Sauté button on Instant Pot. Add ground beef.
2. Cook until brown. Drain, set aside.
3. Drizzle 1 teaspoon coconut oil along bottom of Instant Pot. Add yellow onion, garlic cloves. Cook 1 minute. Add the bell peppers. Sauté until fork tender.
4. Press Keep Warm/Cancel setting to stop Sauté mode.
5. Return ground beef, remaining ingredients, seasoning to Instant Pot. Stir well.
6. Close and seal lid. Press Bean/Chili button. Cook for 30 minutes.
7. Once done, naturally release or quick-release pressure. Open lid carefully. Stir ingredients. (Add more seasoning if desired.)
8. Serve.

10. Weeknight Clam Chowder

Time: 45 minutes

Servings: 4

Ingredients:

- 3 (10-ounce) cans fancy whole baby clams
- 1 pound bacon strips, cooked and crumbled
- 1 Tablespoon butter
- 2 cups chicken broth
- 2 cups heavy cream
- 4 garlic cloves, minced
- 1 red onion, chopped
- 8 ounce package cream cheese
- ¼ cup mozzarella cheese, shredded
- 1 teaspoon ground thyme
- 2 teaspoons salt (to taste)
- 1 teaspoon fresh ground black pepper (to taste)

Instructions:

1. Press Sauté button on Instant Pot. Melt the butter.
2. Add red onion and garlic. Cook/sweat 1 minute.
3. Press Keep Warm/Cancel setting to stop Sauté mode.
4. Add remaining ingredients. Stir well.
5. Close and seal lid. Press Manual setting. Cook on high pressure 30 minutes.
6. Once done, Instant Pot will switch to Keep Warm mode.
7. Remain in Keep Warm mode 5 minutes.
8. Naturally release or quick release the pressure. Open lid carefully. Stir.
9. Serve.

11. Enriching Lamb Stew

Time: 45 minutes

Servings: 4

Ingredients:

- 2 pounds lamb shoulder
- 1 Tablespoon butter
- 1 red onion, chopped
- 4 garlic cloves, minced
- 2 tomatoes, diced
- 3 cups vegetable broth
- 1 (14-ounce) can coconut milk
- 1 teaspoon ginger, grated
- 1 Tablespoon fresh cilantro, chopped
- 1 teaspoon salt
- 1 teaspoon fresh ground black pepper

Instructions:

1. Wash the lamb, pat dry. Cut into chunks.
2. Press Sauté button on Instant Pot. Melt the butter.
3. Add red onion, garlic to Instant Pot. Cook/sweat for 1 minute.
4. Add lamb shoulder. Sear (brown) on all sides.
5. Press Keep Warm/Cancel button to stop Sauté mode.
6. Add tomatoes, vegetable stock, coconut milk, ginger, cilantro, salt and pepper. Stir well.
7. Close and seal lid. Press Meat/Stew button. Cook for 35 minutes.
8. When done, quick-release the pressure. Open lid carefully. Stir ingredients.
9. Serve. Garnish with fresh cilantro.

12. Almost-Famous Chicken Chili

Time: 40 minutes

Servings: 4

Ingredients:

- 1 pound ground chicken
- 1 Tablespoon butter
- 1 yellow onion, diced
- 2 garlic cloves, minced
- 1 red bell pepper, chopped
- 1 green bell pepper, chopped
- 2 celery stalks, chopped
- 1 jalapeno pepper, chopped (optional)
- 1 cup corn kernels
- 1 can (14-ounce) diced tomatoes
- 2 cups chicken broth
- 1 can (6-ounce) tomato paste
- 1 teaspoon ground cumin
- 1 teaspoon smoked paprika
- 1 Tablespoon fresh cilantro, chopped
- 1 teaspoon salt (to taste)
- 1 teaspoon fresh ground black pepper (to taste)

Instructions:

1. Press Sauté button on Instant Pot. Melt the butter.
2. Add onions and garlic. Sweat for 1 minute.
3. Add ground chicken. Sauté until chicken is brown.
4. Add red and green bell peppers, celery, jalapeno, corn, tomatoes. Stir well.
5. Add tomato paste. Stir well. Add chicken broth. Stir well.
6. Add the spices. Stir well.
7. Press Keep Warm/Cancel setting to stop Sauté mode.
8. Close and seal lid. Press Bean/Chili button. Cook for 30 minutes.
9. Once done, naturally release or quick-release pressure. Stir ingredients.
10. Serve.

13. Delicious Broccoli Cheese Soup

Time: 40 minutes

Servings: 4

Ingredients:

- 1 head broccoli, chopped into florets
- 4 garlic cloves, minced
- 3 cups vegetable broth
- 1 cup heavy cream
- 3 cups cheddar cheese, shredded
- 1 teaspoon salt (to taste)
- 1 teaspoon fresh ground black pepper (to taste)

Instructions:

1. In your Instant Pot, add broccoli florets, garlic, vegetable stock, heavy cream, and shredded cheese. Stir well.
2. Close and seal lid. Press Soup button. Cook for 30 minutes.
3. When done, naturally release or quick-release pressure. Open lid carefully. Stir.
4. Serve.

14. Tongue-Kicking Jalapeno Popper Soup

Time: 40 minutes

Servings: 4

Ingredients:

- 2 chicken breasts, boneless, skinless
- 2 Tablespoons coconut oil
- 6 slices of bacon, cooked and crumbled
- 4 jalapeno peppers, finely sliced
(depending on desired heat level, can leave some seeds in, or remove all the seeds)

- 2 Tablespoons butter
- ½ cup cream cheese, softened
- 1 cup heavy cream
- 2 cups chicken broth
- 2 Tablespoons salsa verde (or green sauce)
- ½ cup cheddar cheese, shredded
- ½ cup mozzarella cheese, shredded
- 1 teaspoon garlic powder
- 1 teaspoon salt (to taste)
- 1 teaspoon black pepper (to taste)

Instructions:

1. Rinse the chicken, pat dry.
2. Press Sauté button on Instant Pot. Heat the coconut oil. Add chicken breasts.
3. Cook until chicken breasts cooked through. Remove and shred chicken with fork.
4. Press Keep Warm/Cancel button to stop Sauté mode.
5. Return chicken to Instant Pot. Add rest of ingredients. Stir well.
6. Close and seal lid. Press Soup button. Cook 30 minutes.
7. When timer beeps, naturally or quick-release pressure. Open lid carefully. Stir.
8. Serve.

15. Southwestern Pork Stew

Time: 40 minutes

Servings: 4

Ingredients:

- 1 pound pork shoulder
- 1 red onion, diced

- 2 garlic cloves, minced
- 2 Tablespoons coconut oil
- 6-ounce can sliced mushrooms
- 1 green bell pepper, chopped
- 1 red bell pepper, chopped
- 4 cups beef broth
- Juice from 1 lime
- ½ cup tomato paste
- 2 teaspoons chili powder
- 2 teaspoons ground cumin
- 1 Tablespoon fresh cilantro, chopped
- 1 teaspoon smoked paprika
- 1 teaspoon salt (to taste)
- 1 teaspoon fresh ground black pepper (to taste)

Instructions:

1. Rinse the pork shoulder, pat dry. Cut into chunks.
2. Press Sauté button on Instant Pot. Heat the coconut oil.
3. Add onion, garlic. Sweat for 1 minute. Add pork shoulder. Brown on all sides.
4. Add mushrooms, bell peppers. Sauté until vegetables have softened.
5. Press Keep Warm/Cancel button to stop Sauté mode.
6. Add rest of ingredients. Stir well.
7. Close and seal lid. Press Soup button. Cook for 30 minutes.
8. When timer beeps, quick-release or naturally release pressure. Open lid carefully. Stir ingredients.
9. Serve.

16. Spiced Pumpkin and Sausage Soup

Time: 40 minutes

Servings: 4

Ingredients:

- 1 pound pork sausage, chopped
- 2 cups pumpkin puree (not pie filling)
- 2 cups vegetable broth
- 1 cup heavy cream
- 4 Tablespoons butter
- 1 red onion
- 2 garlic cloves, minced
- 4 slices of bacon, cooked and crumbled
- 1 teaspoon onion powder
- 1 teaspoon ground cumin
- 1 teaspoon cinnamon
- 1 teaspoon ginger, grated
- 1 teaspoon salt (to taste)
- 1 teaspoon fresh ground black pepper (to taste)

Instructions:

1. Cook the bacon, crumble in small pieces. Set aside.
2. Press Sauté button on Instant Pot. Melt the butter.
3. Add onion and garlic. Sweat for 1 minute.
4. Add sausage. Sauté until sausage is brown.
5. Add pumpkin puree. Stir well.
6. Add vegetable stock, heavy cream. Stir well.
7. Add seasoning. Stir well.
8. Press Keep Warm/Cancel setting to stop Sauté mode.
9. Close and seal lid. Press Soup button. Cook for 30 minutes.
10. When done, quick release or naturally release. Open lid carefully. Stir.
11. Top with crumbled bacon. Serve.

17. Autumn Beef and Vegetable Stew

Time: 45 minutes

Servings: 4

Ingredients:

- 1½ pounds stewing beef chunks
- 4 zucchini, chopped
- 2 carrots, chopped
- 2 cups frozen peas
- 4 cups vegetable broth
- 1 Tablespoon coconut oil
- ½ cup ghee
- 1 red onion, chopped
- 4 garlic cloves, minced
- 2 tomatoes, chopped
- 2 Tablespoons ground cumin
- 1 Tablespoon ground ginger
- 1 teaspoon salt (to taste)
- 1 teaspoon fresh ground black pepper (to taste)

Instructions:

1. Press Sauté button on Instant Pot. Heat the coconut oil.
2. Add onions and garlic. Sweat for 1 minute.
3. Add stewing beef. Brown on all sides. Add zucchini, carrots, and peas.
4. Press Keep Warm/Cancel setting to stop Sauté mode.
5. Add ghee. Stir well. Add vegetable stock. Stir well. Add tomatoes, cumin, ginger, salt and pepper. Stir well.
6. Close and seal lid. Press Meat/Stew button. Cook for 35 minutes.
7. When timer beeps, quick-release or naturally release pressure. Open lid carefully. Stir ingredients.
8. Spoon into serving bowls.

18. Splendid Broccoli and Ham Chowder

Time: 50 minutes

Servings: 6

Ingredients:

- 1 head of broccoli
- 1 pound of ham
- 2 Tablespoons coconut oil
- 1 celery stalk, chopped
- 1 yellow onion, chopped
- 4 garlic cloves, minced
- 4 cups vegetable broth
- 1 cup of organic heavy cream
- ¼ cup mozzarella cheese, shredded
- ¼ cup parmesan cheese, shredded
- ¼ cup fresh parsley, chopped
- 1 teaspoon salt (to taste)
- 1 teaspoon fresh ground black pepper (to taste)

Instructions:

1. Rinse the broccoli, chop into florets. Chop ham into chunks.
2. Press Sauté button on Instant Pot. Heat the coconut oil.
3. Add onions and garlic. Sweat for 1 minute.
4. Add celery. Add cauliflower and ham.
5. Sauté until meat is brown and vegetables have softened.
6. Press Keep Warm/Cancel button to stop Sauté mode.
7. Add vegetable stock, heavy cream. Stir well.
8. Add mozzarella cheese, parmesan cheese. Stir well.
9. Close and seal lid. Press Manual button. Cook on High Pressure for 30 minutes.
10. When timer beeps, Instant Pot will switch to Keep Warm mode.
11. Remain on Keep Warm for 10 minutes.
12. When done, use Quick-Release. Open lid carefully. Stir ingredients.
13. Serve.

19. Magnificent Asparagus Stew

Time: 45 minutes

Servings: 4

Ingredients:

- 2 Tablespoons coconut oil
- 1 pound of asparagus
- 1 green bell pepper, chopped
- 1 red bell pepper, chopped
- 2 shallots, chopped
- 4 garlic cloves, minced
- 1 leek, chopped
- 4 cups vegetable broth
- ¼ cup fresh parsley, chopped
- 1 teaspoon salt (to taste)
- 1 teaspoon fresh ground black pepper (to taste)

Instructions:

1. Rinse asparagus, pat dry.
2. Break off woodsy end. Chop asparagus in bite-size pieces.
3. Press Sauté button on Instant Pot. Heat the coconut oil.
4. Add asparagus, bell peppers, shallots, garlic cloves and leeks.
5. Sauté until vegetables have softened.
6. Press Keep Warm/Cancel setting to stop Sauté mode.
7. Add vegetable broth and parsley. Stir well.
8. Close and seal lid. Press Meat/Stew button on Instant Pot. Cook 35 minutes.
9. When time beeps, quick pressure to release. Open lid carefully. Stir ingredients.
10. Serve.

20. Satisfying Turkey Stew

Time: 45 minutes

Servings: 4

Ingredients:

- 4 cups cooked turkey meat, cut in chunks (not ground turkey)
- 4 celery stalks, chopped
- 2 green onions, chopped
- 2 garlic cloves, minced
- 4 carrots, chopped
- 4 cups turkey or vegetable broth
- Zest and juice from ½ lemon
- 2 Tablespoons coconut oil
- 1 Tablespoon coconut flour
- 1 teaspoon salt (to taste)
- 1 teaspoon fresh ground black pepper (to taste)

Instructions:

1. Press Sauté button on Instant Pot. Heat the coconut oil.
2. Add green onions and garlic. Sweat for 1 minute.
3. Add celery and carrots. Sauté until vegetables have softened.
4. Press Keep Warm/Cancel button to end Sauté mode.
5. Add turkey. Stir in coconut flour to coat ingredients.
6. Pour in turkey/vegetable broth, lemon juice, lemon zest, salt, and pepper. Stir.
7. Close and seal lid. Press Meat/Stew button. Cook for 35 minutes.
8. When timer beeps, set to quick pressure release. Open lid carefully. Stir.
9. Spoon into serving bowls. Serve.

Chapter 4: Flavored Beef, Pork, and Lamb

21. Killer Baby Back Ribs

Time: 45 minutes

Servings: 4

Ingredients:

- 1 rack baby back ribs
- 2 Tablespoons soy sauce
- 2 cups beef broth
- 2 Tablespoons granulated Splenda
- 2 Tablespoons coconut oil
- 3 Tablespoons fresh ginger, grated
- 4 garlic cloves, minced
- 1 Tablespoon chili powder
- 1 Tablespoon paprika
- 1 teaspoon ground mustard
- 1 teaspoon low-carb brown sugar
- 1 teaspoon cayenne pepper
- 1 teaspoon onion powder
- 1 teaspoon salt (to taste)
- 1 teaspoon fresh ground black pepper (to taste)

Instructions:

1. In a small bowl, combine ginger, chili powder, paprika, ground mustard, cayenne pepper, onion powder, salt and pepper. Stir well.
2. Add Splenda, brown sugar. Stir well.
3. Rinse the ribs. (You want ribs slightly damp so seasoning will cling.)
4. Rub seasoning mix on both sides of ribs. Place on a flat baking sheet.
5. Pre-heat oven to broil. Place baking sheet under broiler. Broil 5 minutes per side.

6. Press Sauté mode on Instant Pot. Heat coconut oil.
7. Add garlic and ginger. Cook for 1 minute.
8. Add soy sauce and beef broth. Boil for 15 seconds. Stir well.
9. Press Keep Warm/Cancel setting to end Sauté mode.
10. Slice up the rack of ribs into chunks of 4-5 ribs. Place in Instant Pot.
11. Close and seal lid. Press Manual button. Cook on High-Pressure for 35 minutes.
12. When done, release the pressure quickly or naturally. Open lid carefully.
13. Serve.

22. Juicy Brisket

Time: 50 minutes

Servings: 5

Ingredients:

- 2 pounds of brisket
- 2 Tablespoons coconut oil
- 8-ounces low-carb beer
- 2 Tablespoons soy sauce
- 2 Tablespoons Worcestershire sauce
- 1 Tablespoon dry mustard
- 3 Tablespoons tomato paste
- 2 shallots, thinly sliced
- 1 teaspoon of salt (to taste)
- 1 teaspoon fresh ground black pepper (to taste)

Instructions:

1. In a large Ziploc bag, add all the ingredients. Massage the ingredients.
2. Allow to marinate for 2 hours, up to 12 hours.

3. When ready to cook, transfer all ingredients to Instant Pot.
4. Close and seal lid. Press Manual setting. Cook on High-Pressure for 40 minutes.
5. Once done, quick-release or naturally release the pressure. Open lid carefully.
6. Press Sauté mode. Cook until all the liquid evaporates.
7. Remove the brisket. Let it rest for 5 – 15 minutes before slicing.
8. Serve and enjoy!

23. Contest-Winning Lamb Curry

Time: 40 minutes

Servings: 4

Ingredients:

- 1 pound skinless, boneless lamb
- 1 (8-ounce) can diced tomatoes
- 1 Tablespoon fresh ginger, grated
- 4 garlic cloves, minced
- 1 chili, minced
- ½ cup Greek yogurt
- 1 shallot, chopped
- 1 teaspoon ground cumin
- 1 teaspoon turmeric powder
- ¼ cup fresh cilantro, chopped
- 1 teaspoon salt (to taste)
- 1 teaspoon fresh ground black pepper (to taste)

Instructions:

1. Rinse the lamb, pat dry. Cut into chunks.

2. In a large glass dish, combine all the ingredients. Stir well. Cover with plastic wrap. Place glass dish in refrigerator. Allow to marinate for 2 – 8 hours.
3. When ready to cook, transfer lamb mixture to Instant Pot.
4. Close and seal lid. Press Manual button. Cook on High-Pressure for 30 minutes.
5. When done, naturally release the pressure. Open lid carefully.
6. Press Sauté button and allow to boil until sauce has thickened.
7. Serve.

24. Flavorsome Pulled Pork

Time: 45 minutes

Servings: 4

Ingredients:

- 3 pounds boneless pork shoulder
- 2 Tablespoons coconut oil
- 1 teaspoon onion powder
- 1 teaspoon garlic powder
- 1 Tablespoon paprika
- 1 cup beef broth
- 1 teaspoon salt (to taste)
- 1 teaspoon fresh ground black pepper (to taste)

Barbeque Sauce Ingredients:

- 3 Tablespoons low-sugar ketchup
- 4 Tablespoons granulated Splenda
- ¼ cup yellow mustard
- 2 teaspoons hot sauce
- 3 Tablespoons apple cider vinegar

Instructions:

1. In a small bowl, combine onion powder, garlic powder, paprika, salt and pepper. Mix well. Rub seasoning on pork shoulder.
2. Press Sauté mode on Instant Pot. Heat coconut oil.
3. Sear all sides of pork shoulder.
4. In another bowl, combine barbecue sauce ingredients. Stir well.
5. Press Keep Warm/Cancel setting to end Sauté mode.
6. Add the barbecue sauce and beef broth to Instant Pot. Stir well.
7. Close and seal lid. Press Manual button. Cook on high pressure for 35 minutes.
8. When done, quick-release or naturally release pressure. Open lid carefully.
9. Use two forks to pull pork apart.
10. Press Sauté button. Simmer until sauce reduced and clings to pork.
11. Press Keep Warm/Cancel button.
12. Serve.

25. Super Yummy Pork Chops

Time: 25 minutes

Servings: 4

Ingredients:

-   4 boneless pork chops
-   2 Tablespoons coconut oil
-   2 cups beef broth
-   4 garlic cloves, minced
-   1 teaspoon nutmeg
-   1 teaspoon paprika
-   1 teaspoon onion powder
-   1 teaspoon salt
-   1 teaspoon fresh ground black pepper

Instructions:

1. Season the pork chops with spices listed.
2. Press Sauté button on Instant Pot. Heat the coconut oil.
3. Sear pork chops for 2 minutes per side.
4. Press Keep Warm/Cancel button to end Sauté mode.
5. Pour in beef broth.
6. Close and seal lid. Press Poultry button on control panel. Cook for 15 minutes.
7. When done, quick-release the pressure. Open lid carefully.
8. Serve.

26. Hearty Lemon & Garlic Pork

Time: 25 minutes

Servings: 4

Ingredients:

- 4 pork chops, boneless
- 2 cups beef broth
- 3 Tablespoons ghee, melted
- 3 Tablespoons coconut oil
- 1 teaspoon salt
- 1 teaspoon fresh ground black pepper
- Zest and juice from 2 lemons
- 6 garlic cloves, minced
- ¼ cup fresh parsley, chopped

Instructions:

1. Season the pork chops with salt and pepper, lemon juice and zest.
2. Press the Sauté button on your Instant Pot. Heat coconut oil.
3. Sauté garlic for 1 minute. Add pork chops. Sear for 2 minutes per side.
4. Press the Keep Warm/Cancel button to end Sauté mode.

5. Add ghee and beef broth to the Instant Pot.
6. Close and seal lid. Press Poultry button. Cook for 15 minutes.
7. When done, quick-release to release pressure. Open lid carefully. Stir ingredients.
8. Serve.

27. Tasty Thai Beef

Time: 30 minutes

Servings: 6

Ingredients:

- 1 pound of beef, cut into strips
- 1 green bell pepper, chopped
- 1 red bell pepper, chopped
- Zest and juice from 1 lemon
- 2 cups beef broth
- 2 teaspoons ginger, grated
- 4 garlic cloves, minced
- 2 Tablespoons coconut oil
- 1 Tablespoon coconut amino
- 1 cup roasted pecans
- 1 teaspoon salt
- 1 teaspoon fresh ground black pepper

Instructions:

1. Press Sauté button on Instant Pot. Heat the coconut oil.
2. Sauté garlic and ginger for 1 minute.
3. Add beef strips. Sear 1-2 minutes per side.
4. Add bell peppers. Add salt and pepper.
5. Continue cooking until meat is no longer pink.

6. Add coconut amino, pecans, zest and juice from lemon, beef broth. Stir well.
7. Close and seal lid. Press Manual setting. Cook at High Pressure for 15 minutes.
8. When done, naturally release pressure. Open lid carefully.
9. Let it sit for 5 – 10 minutes.
10.   Serve.

28. Flavorful Beef and Tomato Stuffed Squash

Time: 30 minutes

Servings: 4

Ingredients:

- 1 pound of beef, chopped into chunks
- 1 pound butternut squash, peeled and chopped
- 2 Tablespoons coconut oil
- 2 Tablespoons ghee, melted
- 1 green bell pepper, chopped
- 1 yellow bell pepper, chopped
- 2 (14-ounce) cans diced tomatoes
- 4 garlic cloves, minced
- 1 yellow or red onion, chopped
- 1 Tablespoon fresh thyme, chopped
- 1 Tablespoon fresh rosemary, chopped
- 2 Tablespoons fresh parsley, chopped
- 1 teaspoon cayenne pepper
- 1 teaspoon salt
- 1 teaspoon fresh ground black pepper

Instructions:

1. Press Sauté button on Instant Pot. Heat the coconut oil.
2. Add onion and garlic. Sweat for 2 minutes.

3. Add beef chunks, butternut squash, and bell peppers.
4. Sauté until meat is no longer pink and vegetables have softened.
5. Press Keep Warm/Cancel button to end Sauté mode.
6. Add melted ghee, tomatoes, thyme, rosemary, parsley, cayenne pepper, salt and pepper. Stir well.
7. Close and seal lid. Press Manual button. Cook at High Pressure for 20 minutes.
8. When done, quick-release the pressure. Open lid carefully. Stir ingredients. Adjust the seasoning if needed.
9. Serve.

29. Gratifying Meatloaf

Time: 35 minutes

Servings: 4

Ingredients:

- 3 pounds lean ground beef
- 4 garlic cloves, minced
- 1 yellow onion, chopped
- 1 cup mushrooms, chopped
- 3 large eggs
- ½ cup almond flour
- ¼ cup parmesan cheese, grated
- ¼ cup mozzarella cheese, grated
- ¼ cup fresh parsley, chopped
- 2 Tablespoons sugar-free ketchup
- 2 Tablespoons coconut oil
- 2 teaspoons salt
- 2 teaspoons black pepper
- 2 cups of water

Instructions:

1. Cover trivet with aluminum foil.
2. In a large bowl, add and mix all the ingredients (excluding the water) until well combined. Form into a meatloaf.
3. Pour the water in your Instant Pot. Place trivet inside.
4. Place meatloaf on trivet.
5. Close and seal lid. Press Manual button. Cook at High-Pressure for 25 minutes.
6. When done, naturally release the pressure. Open lid carefully.
7. Let the meatloaf rest for 5 minutes before slicing and serve.

30. Lavender Lamb Chops

Time: 25 minutes

Servings: 2

Ingredients:

- 2 lamb chops, boneless
- 2 Tablespoons ghee, melted
- 1 Tablespoon lavender, chopped
- 2 Tablespoons coconut oil
- 2 Tablespoons fresh rosemary, chopped
- Zest and juice from 1 orange
- Zest and juice from 1 lime
- 1 teaspoon garlic powder
- 1 teaspoon salt
- 1 teaspoon fresh ground black pepper
- 2 cups of water

Instructions:

1. Cover trivet with aluminum foil.
2. Press Sauté button on Instant Pot. Heat the coconut oil.

3. Sear lamb chops for 2 minutes per side. Remove and set aside.
4. Press Keep Warm/Cancel button to end Sauté mode.
5. In a bowl, add and mix the ghee, lavender, rosemary, orange juice, orange zest, lime juice, lime zest, and seasonings.
6. Pour 2 cups of water in Instant Pot. Place trivet inside. Set lamb chops on top.
7. Close and seal lid. Press Manual button. Cook at High-Pressure for 15 minutes.
8. When done, quick-release the pressure. Open lid carefully.
9. Serve.

31. Lovely Ginger Beef and Kale

Time: 35 minutes

Servings: 4

Ingredients:

- 1 pound beef, cut into chunks
- 1 bunch of kale, stemmed and chopped
- ½ pound mushrooms, sliced
- 2 cups beef broth
- 1 red onion, chopped
- 4 garlic cloves, minced
- 2 Tablespoons fresh ginger, grated
- 2 Tablespoons coconut oil
- 1 teaspoon paprika
- 1 teaspoon salt
- 1 teaspoon fresh ground black pepper

Instructions:

1. Press Sauté button on Instant Pot. Heat the coconut oil.
2. Add onions and garlic. Sweat for 1 minute.

3. Add beef chunks. Sauté until meat is no longer pink.
4. Press Keep Warm/Cancel setting to end Sauté mode.
5. Add remaining ingredients. Stir well.
6. Close and seal lid. Press Manual button. Cook at High Pressure for 25 minutes.
7. When timer beeps, quick-release or naturally release pressure. Open lid carefully. Stir ingredients. Adjust seasoning if necessary.
8. Serve.

32. Extraordinary Pork Roast

Time: 40 minutes

Servings: 4

Ingredients:

- 2 pounds pork roast
- 1 head cauliflower, chopped into florets
- 1 pound mushrooms, thinly sliced
- 2 Tablespoons coconut oil
- 1 onion, chopped
- 4 garlic cloves, minced
- 2 celery stalks, chopped
- 1 teaspoon salt
- 1 teaspoon fresh ground black pepper
- 2 cups beef broth

Instructions:

1. Press Sauté button on Instant Pot. Heat the coconut oil.
2. Sauté onion and garlic for 1 minute.
3. Season pork roast with salt and pepper. Sear on all sides.
4. Add cauliflower, mushrooms, and celery. Pour in beef broth. Stir.
5. Close and seal lid. Press Manual button. Cook at High Pressure for 30 minutes.

6. When done, naturally release the pressure. Open lid carefully. Stir ingredients.
7. Remove from Instant Pot. Let it sit for 5 – 10 minutes before slicing.
8. Serve.

33. Remarkable Apple Cider Pork Loin

Time: 40 minutes

Servings: 4

Ingredients:

- 4 pound pork loin
- 2 Tablespoons coconut oil
- 1 onion, sliced
- 4 garlic cloves, minced
- 1 cup apple cider
- 1 teaspoon salt
- 1 teaspoon fresh ground black pepper

Instructions:

1. Press Sauté mode on Instant Pot. Heat the coconut oil.
2. Season pork loin with salt and pepper. Sear all sides.
3. Press Keep Warm/Cancel button to end Sauté mode.
4. Pour in apple cider.
5. Close and seal lid. Press Manual button. Cook at High-Pressure 30 minutes.
6. Once done, quick-release the pressure. Open lid carefully.
7. Let the roast rest for 5 – 10 minutes before slicing.
8. Serve.

34. Awe-Inspiring Lamb Roast

Time: 40 minutes

Servings: 4

Ingredients:

- 5 pound boneless leg of lamb, chopped
- 2 cups beef or vegetable broth
- 2 Tablespoons coconut oil
- 1 broccoli head, chopped into florets
- 1 onion, chopped
- 4 garlic cloves, minced
- 1 Tablespoon balsamic vinegar
- 1 teaspoon salt
- 1 teaspoon fresh ground black pepper
- 1 teaspoon fresh ginger, grated
- 1 teaspoon fresh thyme, chopped
- 1 Tablespoon fresh rosemary, chopped

Instructions:

1. Press Sauté button on Instant Pot. Heat the coconut oil.
2. Add the onion, garlic, ginger, thyme, rosemary. Sweat for 1 minute.
3. Season lamb with salt and pepper. Sear on all sides.
4. Press Keep Warm/Cancel button to end Sauté mode.
5. Add balsamic vinegar and beef broth. Stir well.
6. Close and seal cover. Press Manual switch. Cook at High Pressure for 30 minutes.
7. When done, quick-release pressure. Open lid carefully.
8. Let the roast rest for 5 – 10 minutes before slicing.
9. Serve.

35. Melt-In-Your-Mouth Salisbury Steak

Time: 35 minutes

Servings: 4

Steak Ingredients:

- 2 pounds lean ground beef
- 1 Tablespoon coconut oil
- ½ yellow onion, diced
- 2 garlic cloves, minced
- 1 Tablespoon bread crumbs
- 1 egg
- ¼ cup coconut flour
- ¼ cup beef broth
- 1 Tablespoon Worcestershire sauce
- 1 Tablespoon fresh parsley, chopped
- 1 teaspoon salt
- 1 teaspoon fresh ground black pepper

Gravy Ingredients:

- 2 Tablespoons ghee, melted
- 2 cups mushrooms, sliced
- 1 onion, sliced
- ½ cup beef broth
- ¼ cup sour cream
- 2 Tablespoons fresh parsley, chopped
- 1 Tablespoon tomato paste
- 1 teaspoon Worcestershire sauce
- 1 teaspoon salt
- 1 teaspoon fresh ground black pepper

Instructions:

1. In a large bowl, mix steak ingredients, except coconut oil.
2. Shape into round patties, ¼ inch thick. Set aside.
3. Press Sauté button on Instant Pot. Heat the coconut oil.

4. Cook patties 2 minutes per side, until golden brown.
5. Remove patties. Set aside.
6. Heat the ghee. Add gravy ingredients. Stir well.
7. Press Keep Warm/Cancel button to end Sauté mode.
8. Return patties to Instant Pot.
9. Close and seal cover. Press Manual switch. Cook at High Pressure for 25 minutes.
10. When done, quick-release pressure. Open lid carefully.
11. Serve.

Chapter 5: Mouth-Watering Seafood and Chicken

36. Spicy Spirited Lemon Salmon

Time: 20 minutes

Servings: 4

Ingredients:

- 4 salmon fillets
- Juice from 2 lemons + slices for garnish
- 1 cup of water
- 1 Tablespoon paprika
- 1 teaspoon cayenne pepper
- 1 teaspoon salt (to taste)
- 1 teaspoon fresh ground black pepper (to taste)

Instructions:

1. Rinse the salmon, pat dry.
2. In a bowl, combine salt, pepper, paprika, cayenne pepper.
3. Drizzle lemon juice over salmon fillet. Season with spice mixture. Turn over fillet, repeat on other side.
4. Add 1 cup of water to Instant Pot. Place trivet inside. Place fillets on trivet.
5. Close and seal cover. Press Manual button. Cook at High-Pressure for 10 minutes.
6. Once done, quick-release pressure. Open lid carefully.
7. Serve.

37. Awesome Coconut Shrimp Curry

Time: 35 minutes

Servings: 4

Ingredients:

- 1 pound shrimp, peeled and deveined
- 1 Tablespoon coconut oil
- 4 garlic cloves, minced
- Juice from 1 lime
- 1 teaspoon salt
- 1 teaspoon fresh ground black pepper
- 4 tomatoes, chopped
- 1 red bell pepper, sliced
- 10-ounces coconut milk
- ½ cup fresh cilantro, chopped

Instructions:

1. Press Sauté mode on Instant Pot. Heat the coconut oil
2. Season shrimp with lime juice, salt and pepper.
3. Sauté garlic for 1 minute.
4. Add shrimp. Cook 2 – 4 minutes per side.
5. Add bell peppers and tomatoes. Stir well.
6. Press Keep Warm/Cancel button to cancel Sauté mode.
7. Add coconut milk. Stir well.
8. Close and seal lid. Press Manual setting. Cook at High Pressure for 25 minutes.
9. Once done, quick-release pressure. Open lid carefully.
10. Garnish with fresh cilantro. Serve.

38. Wondrous Mediterranean Fish

Time: 25 minutes

Servings: 4

Ingredients:

- 4 fish fillets (any kind)
- 1 pound cherry tomatoes, halved
- 1 cup green olives, pitted
- 2 garlic cloves, minced
- 1 cup of water
- 1 teaspoon coconut oil
- 1 Tablespoon fresh thyme, chopped
- 1 teaspoon fresh parsley
- 1 teaspoon salt (to taste)
- 1 teaspoon fresh ground black pepper (to taste)

Instructions:

1. Pour 1 cup of water in Instant Pot. Cover trivet in foil.
2. On a flat surface, rub fish fillets with garlic. Season with salt, pepper and thyme.
3. Place olives and cherry tomatoes along bottom of Instant Pot.
4. Place fillets on trivet.
5. Close and seal lid. Press Manual button. Cook at High Pressure for 15 minutes.
6. When done, release pressure naturally. Open lid carefully.
7. Place the fish with the ingredients. Stir to coat them.
8. Plate the fillets. Top with fresh parsley.
9. Serve.

39. Wild Alaskan Cod

Time: 25 minutes

Servings: 4

Ingredients:

- 4 wild Alaskan cod fillets
- 4 cups cherry tomatoes, halved
- 4 garlic cloves, minced
- 4 Tablespoons butter, melted
- 1 Tablespoon coconut oil
- ¼ cup of fresh cilantro, chopped
- 1 teaspoon salt (to taste)
- 1 teaspoon fresh ground black pepper (to taste)

Instructions:

1. On a flat surface, rub garlic over cod fillets. Season with salt and pepper.
2. Cover trivet with foil.
3. Add 1 cup of water to Instant Pot. Place trivet inside.
4. Place tomatoes along bottom of Instant Pot. Season with salt and pepper.
5. Place salmon fillets on trivet.
6. Pour melted butter and coconut oil over cod fillets and tomatoes.
7. Close and seal lid. Press Manual switch. Cook at High Pressure for 15 minutes.
8. When timer beeps, quick-release pressure. Open lid carefully.
9. Plate the fillets. Top with tomatoes and fresh cilantro.
10.   Serve.

40. Stunning Shrimp and Sausage Gumbo

Time: 35 minutes

Servings: 4

Ingredients:

- 1 pound shrimp, peeled and deveined
- 1 pound lean sausage, thinly sliced
- 1 red bell pepper, chopped
- 1 yellow onion, chopped
- 1 garlic clove, minced
- 1 celery stalk, chopped
- 2 cups chicken broth
- ½ cup fresh parsley, chopped
- 2 Tablespoons coconut oil
- 2 Tablespoons Cajun seasoning
- 1 teaspoon salt (to taste)
- 1 teaspoon fresh ground black pepper (to taste)

Instructions:

1. Press Sauté button on Instant Pot. Heat the coconut oil.
2. Sauté onion and garlic for 1 minute.
3. Add sausage and shrimp. Cook until golden brown.
4. Add bell pepper and celery. Season with Cajun spice. Stir well.
5. Press Keep Warm/Cancel setting to stop Sauté mode.
6. Add 2 cups of chicken broth. Stir well.
7. Close and seal lid. Press Meat/Stew button. Adjust to cook for 25 minutes.
8. When timer beeps, quick-release or naturally release pressure. Open lid carefully. Stir well.
9. Serve.

41. Appetizing Steamed Crab Legs

Time: 20 minutes

Servings: 4

Ingredients:

- 2 pounds frozen crab legs
- 2 cups of water
- 4 Tablespoons butter, melted
- Juice from 1 lemon
- 1 teaspoon salt (to taste)
- 1 teaspoon fresh ground black pepper (to taste)

Instructions:

1. In a small bowl, combine melted butter, lemon juice, salt and pepper.
2. Add 2 cups of water to Instant Pot. Cover trivet in foil.
3. Place trivet in Instant Pot.
4. Place crab legs in single layer on trivet. Pour half butter mixture over crab.
5. Close and seal lid. Press Manual button. Cook at High Pressure for 10 minutes.
6. When done, quick-release the pressure. Open lid carefully.
7. Plate the crab legs. Pour remaining butter mixture over crab.
8. Serve.

42. Mouthwatering Parmesan Cod

Time: 30 minutes

Servings: 4

Ingredients:

- 4 cod fillets
- 4 green onions, minced
- 4 garlic cloves, minced
- ½ cup of parmesan cheese, grated
- 1 cup low-carb mayonnaise
- 1 teaspoon Worcestershire sauce
- 2 cups of water
- 1 teaspoon salt (to taste)
- 1 teaspoon fresh ground black pepper (to taste)

Instructions:

1. Add 2 cups of water in Instant Pot. Cover trivet with foil.
2. In a bowl, add green onions, garlic cloves, parmesan cheese, mayonnaise, Worcestershire sauce, salt, and black pepper. Stir well.
3. Coat cod fillets with mixture. Place on trivet.
4. Close and seal lid. Press Manual button. Cook at High Pressure for 20 minutes.
5. Once done, quick-release pressure. Open lid carefully.
6. Let the cod rest for 5 minutes before removing.
7. Serve.

43. Lovely Tilapia Fillets

Time: 25 minutes

Servings: 4

Ingredients:

- 4 boneless, tilapia fillets
- ½ cup parmesan cheese, grated
- 4 Tablespoons low-carb mayonnaise
- ¼ cup ghee, melted
- 2 cups of water
- 1 teaspoon fresh basil, chopped
- 1 teaspoon onion powder
- Juice from ½ lemon
- 1 teaspoon garlic powder
- 1 teaspoon salt (to taste)
- 1 teaspoon fresh ground black pepper (to taste)

Instructions:

1. Pour 2 cups of water in Instant Pot. Cover trivet with foil.
2. In a bowl, combine parmesan cheese, mayonnaise, ghee, basil, lemon juice, and seasonings.
3. Coat tilapia fillets with mixture. Place the tilapia fillets on trivet.
4. Close and seal lid. Press Manual button. Cook at High Pressure for 15 minutes.
5. Once done, quick-release pressure. Open lid carefully.
6. Allow the fish to rest for 5 minutes before removing.
7. Serve.

44. Generous Orange Trout Fillets

Time: 25 minutes

Servings: 4

Ingredients:

- 4 trout fillets
- 4 garlic cloves
- Zest and juice from 1 orange
- ¼ cup fresh parsley, chopped
- 1 cup pecans, roasted and chopped
- 1 Tablespoon ghee
- 2 cups of water
- 1 Tablespoon coconut oil
- 1 teaspoon salt (to taste)
- 1 teaspoon fresh ground black pepper (to taste)

Instructions:

1. Pour 2 cups of water in Instant Pot. Cover trivet with foil.
2. In a bowl, combine orange juice and zest, garlic, parsley, ghee, coconut oil, salt, and pepper. Stir well.
3. Cover trout with mixture. Place trout fillets on trivet.
4. Close and seal lid. Press Manual button. Cook at High-Pressure for 15 minutes.
5. Once done, quick-release pressure. Open lid carefully.
6. Plate the fillets. Serve.

45. Intriguing Oysters

Time: 30 minutes

Servings: 4

Ingredients:

- 1 pound oysters, shucked
- 4 garlic cloves, minced
- ¼ cup fresh parsley, chopped
- 1 teaspoon paprika
- Juice from 1 lemon + slices for garnish
- 2 Tablespoons ghee, melted
- 2 cups of water
- 1 teaspoon salt (to taste)
- 1 teaspoon fresh ground black pepper (to taste)

Instructions:

1. Rinse the oysters.
2. In a bowl, combine garlic, parsley, paprika, lemon juice, ghee, salt, and black pepper.
3. Place the oysters in Instant Pot. Pour mixture over the oysters.
4. Close and seal the lid. Press Manual setting. Cook at High Pressure 20 minutes.
5. When done, quick-release pressure. Open lid carefully.
6. Serve. Top with lemon wedges.

46. Robust Halibut Fillets

Time: 30 minutes

Servings: 4

Ingredients:

- 4 halibut fillets
- 6 garlic cloves, minced
- 4 green onions, chopped
- ¼ cup low-carb mayonnaise
- ¼ cup ghee, melted
- ¼ cup fresh parmesan cheese, grated
- ¼ cup mozzarella cheese, grated
- 1 teaspoon salt (to taste)
- 1 teaspoon fresh ground black pepper (to taste)
- Zest and juice from 1 lime
- 2 cups of water
- 1 lemon sliced for garnish
- Fresh parsley for garnish

Instructions:

1. Pour 2 cups of water in Instant Pot. Cover trivet with foil.
2. In a large mixing bowl, add the garlic, green onions, mayonnaise, ghee, cheeses, lime juice, lime zest, salt, and pepper. Stir well.
3. Coat the halibut fillets with the mixture. Place halibut on trivet.
4. Close and seal lid. Press Manual button. Cook at High-Pressure for 20 minutes.
5. Once done, quick-release or naturally release pressure> Open lid carefully.
6. Plate the halibut. Top with fresh parsley, lemon slices. Serve.

47. Fantastic Chili Lime Cod

Time: 30 minutes

Servings: 4

Ingredients:

- 4 cod fillets, shredded
- 1 can (14-oucne) diced tomatoes
- 4 garlic cloves, minced
- 1 celery stalk, chopped
- 1 yellow onion, chopped
- 1 Tablespoon rice wine vinegar
- ½ cup low-carb mayonnaise
- ¼ cup fresh parsley, chopped
- Zest and juice from 1 lime
- 1 cup vegetable stock
- 1 Tablespoon coconut oil
- 1 teaspoon paprika
- 1 teaspoon salt
- 1 teaspoon fresh ground black pepper

Instructions:

1. Press Sauté mode on Instant Pot. Heat the coconut oil.
2. Add onion and garlic. Sauté for 1 minute. Add the celery and shredded cod.
3. Press Keep Warm/Cancel setting to stop Sauté mode.
4. Add diced tomatoes, mayonnaise, rice wine vinegar, parsley, lime juice, lime zest, and seasoning. Stir well.
5. Close and seal lid. Press Manual switch. Cook at High Pressure for 20 minutes.
6. Once done, quickly or naturally release pressure. Open lid carefully. Stir.
7. Serve.

48. Delicious Cauliflower Risotto and Salmon

Time: 30 minutes

Servings: 4

Ingredients:

- 4 salmon fillets, shredded
- 1 pound asparagus, stemmed and chopped
- 1 head cauliflower, chopped into florets
- 8-ounce coconut cream, unsweetened
- 1 Tablespoon fresh or dried rosemary, chopped
- 2 teaspoons fresh or dried thyme, chopped
- ½ cup parmesan cheese, shredded
- 1 cup chicken broth
- 1 Tablespoon coconut oil
- 2 teaspoons salt (to taste)
- 1 teaspoon fresh ground black pepper (to taste)

Instructions:

1. In a food processor, add cauliflower florets. Pulse until rice-like consistency. Remove and set aside.
2. Press Sauté button on Instant Pot. Add the coconut oil, cauliflower rice, asparagus, and shredded salmon fillet. Cook until light brown and tender.
3. Press the Keep Warm/Cancel setting to stop the Sauté mode.
4. Add remaining ingredients. Stir well.
5. Close and seal lid. Press Manual button. Cook at High Pressure for 20 minutes.
6. Once done, naturally or quick-release pressure. Open lid carefully. Stir well.
7. Serve.

49. Tender Ginger Sesame Glaze Salmon

Time: 25 minutes

Servings: 4

Ingredients:

- 4 salmon fillets
- 4 garlic cloves, minced
- 1 Tablespoon fish sauce
- 1 Tablespoon fresh ginger, grated
- 1 Tablespoon sugar-free ketchup
- 2 Tablespoons white wine
- 1 Tablespoon rice vinegar
- 2 Tablespoons soy sauce
- 2 teaspoons sesame oil
- 2 cups of water

Instructions:

1. In a bowl, combine garlic, fish sauce, ginger, ketchup, white wine, rice vinegar, soy sauce, and sesame oil.
2. In a large Ziploc bag, add the sauce and salmon fillets. Marinate for 6 – 10 hours.
3. Pour 2 cups of water in Instant Pot. Cover trivet in foil. Place trivet in Instant Pot.
4. Place marinated salmon fillet on trivet.
5. Close and seal lid. Press Manual button. Cook at High Pressure for 15 minutes.
6. Once done, naturally release pressure. Open lid carefully.
7. Serve.

50. Supreme Chicken Breasts

Time: 20 minutes

Servings: 4

Ingredients:

- 4 chicken breasts, boneless, skinless
- 2 Tablespoons coconut oil
- 1 teaspoon salt (to taste)
- 1 teaspoon fresh ground black pepper (to taste)
- 2 cups of water

Instructions:

1. Cover trivet with foil.
2. Press Sauté button on Instant Pot. Heat the coconut oil.
3. Season the chicken with salt and pepper. Sauté for 2 minutes per side, until a golden crust forms. Remove chicken breasts and set aside.
4. Press Keep Warm/Cancel setting to end Sauté mode.
5. Pour 2 cups of water in the Instant Pot. Place trivet inside.
6. Place chicken breasts on trivet.
7. Close and seal lid. Press Manual button. Cook at High Pressure for 10 minutes.
8. When done, naturally release pressure. Open lid carefully. Let chicken rest for 5 minutes in Instant Pot.
9. Plate and serve.

51. Delicious Cheesy Spinach Stuffed Chicken Breasts

Time: 20 minutes

Servings: 2

Ingredients:

- 2 chicken breasts
- 1 red bell pepper, chopped
- 1 cup mozzarella cheese, shredded
- 1 cup parmesan cheese, shredded
- 3 Tablespoons coconut oil
- 2 cups baby spinach
- 1 teaspoon garlic powder
- 1 teaspoon onion powder
- 1 teaspoon salt (to taste)
- 1 teaspoon fresh ground black pepper (to taste)
- 2 cups of water

Instructions:

1. Cover trivet with foil.
2. Press Sauté button on Instant Pot. Heat 2 tablespoons of the coconut oil.
3. Sauté the chicken until golden brown on both sides.
4. Remove the chicken breasts and allow to cool.
5. Press Keep Warm/Cancel button to end Sauté mode.
6. In a large bowl, combine red pepper, parmesan cheese, mozzarella cheese, 1 tablespoon of coconut oil, baby spinach, and seasoning.
7. When chicken is cool, cut down middle, but don't cut all the way through.
8. Stuff with spinach mixture.
9. Pour 2 cups of water in Instant Pot. Place trivet inside. Place chicken on trivet.
10. Close and seal lid. Press Manual button. Cook at High Pressure for 7 minutes.
11. When done, naturally release pressure. Open lid carefully.
12. Allow chicken to rest 5 minutes.
13. Plate and serve.

52. Royal Lemon Pepper Chicken

Time: 25 minutes

Servings: 4

Ingredients:

- 4 chicken breasts, skinless, boneless
- 2 Tablespoons coconut oil
- 2 Tablespoons butter, melted
- Zest and juice from 2 lemons
- 2 teaspoons salt (to taste)
- 1 Tablespoon lemon pepper seasoning (to taste)
- 2 Tablespoons fresh parsley, chopped

Instructions:

1. Press Sauté button on Instant Pot. Heat the coconut oil.
2. Sauté the chicken. Cook until golden brown on each side.
3. Press Keep Warm/Cancel setting to end Sauté mode.
4. In a bowl, add melted butter, lemon juice, lemon zest, salt, lemon pepper seasoning, and parsley. Stir well.
5. Coat chicken with seasoning mixture. Return chicken to Instant Pot.
6. Close and seal lid. Press Manual button. Cook at High Pressure for 5 minutes.
7. When done, naturally release pressure. Open lid carefully.
8. Allow chicken to rest for 5 minutes.
9. Serve.

53. Flaming Buffalo Chicken Strips

Time: 20 minutes

Servings: 2

Ingredients:

- 2 chicken breasts, boneless, skinless
- 1 cup of water
- 1 Tablespoon low-carb barbecue sauce
- 1 Tablespoon cayenne pepper
- 1 Tablespoon dried oregano
- 1 teaspoon garlic powder
- 1 teaspoon ground cumin
- 1 teaspoon chili powder
- 1 Tablespoon coconut oil
- 1 teaspoon salt (to taste)
- 1 teaspoon fresh ground black pepper (to taste)

Instructions:

1. Cover trivet in foil.
2. Press Sauté button on Instant Pot. Heat the coconut oil.
3. Add the chicken. Cook until brown on each side.
4. Remove the chicken breasts and set aside.
5. Press Keep Warm/Cancel setting to end Sauté mode.
6. Season chicken with barbecue sauce, spices, and seasonings.
7. Pour water in Instant Pot. Place trivet in pot. Place chicken on trivet.
8. Close and seal lid. Press Manual button. Cook at High Pressure for 8 minutes.
9. When done, naturally release pressure. Open lid carefully.
10. Allow chicken to rest for 5 minutes.
11. Serve.

54. Succulent Garlic Paprika Chicken Legs with Green Beans

Time: 20 minutes

Servings: 4

Ingredients:

- 4 chicken drumsticks
- 1 pound green beans, trimmed and chopped
- 1 cup chicken broth
- 1 Tablespoon coconut oil
- 2 Tablespoons onion powder
- 4 Tablespoons fresh herbs, chopped (rosemary, oregano, thyme)
- 1 Tablespoon smoked paprika
- 1 teaspoon salt
- 1 teaspoon fresh ground black pepper

Instructions:

1. In a bowl, combine fresh herbs and seasonings. Stir well.
2. In a large Ziploc bag, add chicken drumsticks and seasoning mixture.
3. Allow to marinate in refrigerator for 6 hours or overnight.
4. When ready to cook. Press Sauté button on Instant Pot. Heat the coconut oil.
5. Add the drumsticks. Cook until a golden crust forms.
6. Press Keep Warm/Cancel setting to end Sauté mode.
7. Add green beans and chicken broth to Instant Pot.
8. Close and seal lid. Press Manual button. Cook at High Pressure for 10 minutes.
9. When done, quick-release or naturally release pressure. Open lid carefully.
10. Allow chicken to rest for 5 minutes before removing.
11. Serve.

55. Phenomenal Whole Rotisserie Chicken

Time: 30 minutes

Servings: 6

Ingredients:

- 1 whole chicken
- Zest and juice from 1 lemon
- 2 cups chicken broth
- 2 Tablespoons coconut oil
- 2 teaspoons salt
- 2 teaspoons fresh ground black pepper
- 2 teaspoons paprika
- 2 Tablespoons fresh herbs, chopped
- 4 garlic cloves, minced

Instructions:

1. Remove any parts included inside chicken cavity. Rinse and pat dry.
2. In a bowl, combine the seasoning and herbs.
3. Pour coconut oil over the chicken. Rub seasoning mixture into chicken skin.
4. Press Sauté button on Instant Pot.
5. Place chicken in Instant Pot. Sauté all sides for 5 minutes.
6. Press Keep Warm/Cancel setting to stop Sauté mode.
7. Add chicken broth.
8. Close and seal lid. Press Manual switch. Cook at High Pressure for 25 minutes.
9. When done, naturally release pressure. Open lid carefully.
10. Allow to rest for 5 minutes before removing.
11. Serve.

Chapter 6: Vegan and Vegetarian

56. Unbelievable Zucchini with Avocado Sauce

Time: 15 minutes

Servings: 4

Ingredients:

- 2 pounds of zucchini, chopped
- 2 avocados, chopped
- Juice from 1 lime
- 1 shallot, chopped
- 2 garlic cloves, minced
- 1 cup of water
- 2 Tablespoons coconut oil
- ¼ cup fresh basil, chopped
- 1 teaspoon salt (to taste)
- 1 teaspoon fresh ground black pepper (to taste)

Instructions:

1. Press Sauté mode on Instant Pot. Heat the coconut oil.
2. Sauté garlic and shallots for 1 minute.
3. Press Keep Warm/Cancel setting to stop Sauté mode.
4. Add zucchini, avocado, basil, salt, and black pepper. Stir well.
5. Add the water. Stir well.
6. Close and seal lid. Press Manual setting. Cook at High-Pressure for 5 minutes.
7. Quick release or naturally release pressure. Open lid carefully. Stir ingredients.
8. Allow to cool down or refrigerate overnight.

57. Awesome Vegan Patties

Time: 15 minutes

Servings: 2

Ingredients:

- 2 cups mushrooms, chopped
- 1 onion, chopped
- 2 garlic cloves, minced
- 1 cup vegetable broth
- 1 Tablespoon ghee, melted
- 2 Tablespoons fresh basil, chopped
- 1 Tablespoon fresh oregano, chopped
- 1 teaspoon salt
- 1 teaspoon fresh ground black pepper
- 1 teaspoon fresh ginger, grated
- 2 ketogenic hamburger buns (to serve)
- 1 cup mixed lettuce (topping)

Instructions:

1. Press Sauté button on Instant Pot. Cover trivet in foil.
2. Add melted ghee, garlic cloves, onion, mushrooms, and ginger. Sauté until vegetables become translucent.
3. Press Keep Warm/Cancel setting to stop Sauté mode.
4. Add vegetable stock, basil, oregano, salt, and black pepper. Stir well.
5. Close and seal lid. Press Manual switch. Cook at High Pressure for 6 minutes.
6. When timer goes off, quick-release pressure. Allow to cool.
7. Once completely cooled, mash ingredients with a fork or masher until smooth. Form into patties.
8. Pour 2 cups of water in Instant Pot. Place trivet inside. Place patties on trivet.
9. Close and seal lid. Press Manual button. Cook at High Pressure for 7 minutes.

10.   Serve.

58. Scrumptious Brussel Sprouts

Time: 15 minutes

Servings: 4

Ingredients:

- 1 pound Brussel sprouts
- 2 Tablespoons coconut oil
- 1 teaspoon salt
- 1 teaspoon fresh ground black pepper

Instructions:

1. Add 2 cups of water in Instant Pot. Place trivet in Instant Pot. Place steamer basket on top.
2. Add Brussel sprouts to steamer basket. Drizzle with coconut oil; sprinkle with salt and black pepper.
3. Close and seal lid. Press Manual switch. Cook at High Pressure for 7 minutes.
4. When done, quickly release pressure. Open lid carefully.
5. Serve.

59. Wonderful Eggplant Lasagna

Time: 30 minutes

Servings: 4

Ingredients:

- 1 pound of eggplant, sliced
- 4 garlic cloves, minced
- 2 Tablespoons coconut oil
- Juice from 1 lemon
- 1 cup vegetable broth
- 6 cups low-carb tomato sauce
- 1 cup mozzarella cheese, shredded
- 1 cup parmesan cheese, grated
- 1 cup ricotta cheese
- 1 Tablespoon fresh basil leaves, chopped
- 1 Tablespoon fresh oregano, chopped
- 1 Tablespoon paprika
- 1 teaspoon salt
- 1 teaspoon fresh ground black pepper

Instructions:

1. Grease a baking dish with non-stick cooking spray.
2. In a bowl, combine the cheeses and herbs.
3. In a separate bowl, add and season the eggplants with garlic cloves, lemon juice, paprika, salt, and black pepper.
4. Layer baking dish with eggplant slices, tomato sauce. Sprinkle mixed cheeses. Repeat.
5. Cover baking dish with aluminum foil.
6. Add 2 cups of water. Place trivet in Instant Pot. Place dish on trivet.
7. Close and seal lid. Press Manual switch. Cook at High Pressure for 25 minutes.
8. When done, naturally release or quickly release pressure. Open lid carefully.

9. Serve.

60. Won't Know It's Vegan Chili

Time: 35 minutes

Servings: 4

Ingredients:

- 1 eggplant, chopped
- 1 jalapeno, chopped
- 1 red bell pepper, chopped
- 1 green bell pepper, chopped
- 1 zucchini, chopped
- 4 garlic cloves, minced
- 1 onion, chopped
- ½ pound mushrooms, chopped
- 2 Tablespoons coconut oil
- 2 cups vegetable broth
- 1 can (6-ounce) tomato paste
- 1 can (14-oucne) diced tomatoes
- 1 Tablespoon Chili powder
- 1 teaspoon ground cumin
- 1 teaspoon salt (to taste)
- 1 teaspoon fresh ground black pepper (to taste)

Instructions:

1. Press Sauté button on Instant Pot. Heat the coconut oil.
2. Add eggplant, jalapeno, bell peppers, zucchinis, garlic cloves, onion, and mushrooms. Sauté until vegetables become soft.
3. Press Keep Warm/Cancel setting to stop Sauté mode.
4. Add tomato paste. Stir well.
5. Add vegetable broth, diced tomatoes, and seasonings. Stir well.

6. Close and seal lid. Press Bean/Chili button. Cook for 30 minutes.
7. Once cooking done, naturally release or quick-release pressure.
8. Stir chili. Adjust seasoning if necessary.
9. Serve.

61. Buddha's Tofu and Broccoli Delight

Time: 15 minutes

Servings: 4

Ingredients:

- 1 pound of tofu, extra firm, chopped into cubes
- 1 broccoli head, chopped into florets
- 1 onion, chopped
- 1 carrot, chopped
- 4 garlic cloves, minced
- 2 Tablespoons low-carb brown sugar
- 1 Tablespoon fresh ginger, grated
- 1 Tablespoon rice vinegar
- 1 cup vegetable broth
- 2 scallions, chopped
- 2 Tablespoons coconut oil
- 1 teaspoon salt (to taste)
- 1 teaspoon fresh ground black pepper (to taste)

Instructions:

1. Press Sauté button on Instant Pot. Heat the coconut oil.
2. Sauté garlic and onion for 2 minutes.
3. Add broccoli florets and tofu. Sauté for 3 minutes.
4. Press Keep Warm/Cancel button to end Sauté mode.
5. Add remaining ingredients. Stir well.

6. Close and seal lid. Press Manual setting. Cook at High Pressure for 6 minutes.
7. When timer beeps, quick-release pressure. Open lid carefully.
8. Serve.

62. Special Spicy Almond Tofu

Time: 25 minutes

Servings: 4

Ingredients:

- 1 pound extra firm tofu, chopped into cubes
- 1 cauliflower head, chopped into florets
- 1 broccoli head, chopped into florets
- 1 cup almonds, roughly chopped
- 2 Tablespoons low-carb soy sauce
- 2 Tablespoons green Chili Sauce
- 2 Tablespoons coconut oil
- 1 teaspoon garlic powder
- 1 teaspoon onion powder
- 1 teaspoon salt (to taste)
- 1 teaspoon fresh ground black pepper (to taste)

Instructions:

1. Press Sauté button on Instant Pot. Heat the coconut oil.
2. Add tofu, cauliflower florets, and broccoli florets. Sauté until fork tender.
3. Press Keep Warm/Cancel setting to end Sauté mode.
4. Add remaining ingredients to Instant Pot. Stir well.
5. Close and seal lid. Press Manual switch. Cook at High Pressure for 10 minutes.

6. When timer beeps, naturally release or quickly release pressure. Open lid carefully. Stir ingredients.
7. Serve.

63. Fresh Garlic Cauliflower and Sweet Potato Mash

Time: 20 minutes

Servings: 4

Ingredients:

- 2 pounds sweet potatoes, chopped
- 1 head cauliflower, chopped into florets
- 4 garlic cloves, minced
- 2 Tablespoons coconut oil
- 1 teaspoon salt (to taste)
- 1 teaspoon fresh ground black pepper (to taste)
- 2 cups of water

Instructions:

1. Press Sauté button on Instant Pot. Heat the coconut oil.
2. Sauté sweet potatoes, cauliflower, and garlic. Sauté until almost tender.
3. Press Keep Warm/Cancel button to end Sauté mode.
4. Add the water to your ingredients.
5. Close and seal lid. Press Manual switch. Cook at High Pressure for 10 minutes.
6. When timer beeps, quick-release pressure. Mash ingredients in Pot until smooth.
7. Serve.

64. Everyday Bold Beet and Caper Salad

Servings: 2

Time: 30 minutes

Ingredients:

- 4 beets, sliced
- 4 carrots, sliced
- 1 cup pine nuts, chopped
- 2 Tablespoons rice wine vinegar
- 1 cup of water

Dressing Ingredients:

- 1 Tablespoon coconut oil, melted and cooled
- ¼ cup fresh parsley, chopped
- 2 garlic cloves, minced
- 2 Tablespoons capers
- 4-ounces goat cheese, crumbled
- 1 teaspoon salt
- 1 teaspoon fresh ground black pepper

Instructions:

1. Pour 1 cup of water in Instant Pot.
2. Place a trivet inside; place steamer basket on top.
3. Add sliced beets, pine nuts, and carrots to steamer basket.
4. Drizzle with rice wine vinegar.
5. Close and seal lid. Press Manual setting. Cook at High Pressure for 20 minutes.
6. As it cooks, in a large bowl, combine dressing ingredients. Stir well. Set aside.
7. When done, naturally release pressure. Open lid carefully.
8. In a large bowl, combine the beets and carrots with dressing. Stir until coated.
9. Serve.

65. Fragrant Zucchini Mix

Servings: 4

Time: 15 minutes

Ingredients:

- 2 pounds zucchini, roughly chopped
- 1 broccoli head, chopped into florets
- 1 red onion, chopped
- 2 garlic cloves, minced
- 2 Tablespoons coconut oil
- 1 cup of water
- 2 cups fresh basil, chopped
- 1 teaspoon salt (to taste)
- 1 teaspoon fresh ground black pepper (to tastes)

Instructions:

1. Press Sauté button on Instant Pot. Heat the coconut oil.
2. Sauté onion and garlic for 1 minute.
3. Add broccoli florets and zucchini. Sauté until the vegetables become soft.
4. Press Keep Warm/Cancel setting to end Sauté mode.
5. Add remaining ingredients to vegetables. Stir well.
6. Close and seal lid. Press Manual switch. Cook at High Pressure for 7 minutes.
7. When timer goes off, quick-release pressure. Open lid carefully.
8. Serve.

66. Not Your Average Mushroom Risotto

Time: 15 minutes

Servings: 2

Ingredients:

- 2 pounds cremini mushrooms, chopped
- 1 pound extra firm tofu, chopped into cubes
- Bunch of baby spinach, freshly chopped
- 1 Tablespoon ghee
- 1 Tablespoon nutritional yeast
- 4 garlic cloves, minced
- ⅓ cup parmesan cheese, shredded
- 1 red onion, chopped
- 2 Tablespoons coconut oil
- ¼ cup dry white wine
- 3 cups vegetable broth
- Zest and juice from 1 lemon
- 1 teaspoon fresh thyme, chopped
- 1 teaspoon salt (to taste)
- 1 teaspoon fresh ground black pepper (to taste)

Instructions:

1. Press Sauté button on Instant Pot. Melt the ghee.
2. Sauté garlic and onion for 1 minute.
3. Add tofu and mushrooms. Cook until softened.
4. Press Keep Warm/Cancel button to end Sauté mode.
5. Add remaining ingredients. Stir well.
6. Close and seal lid. Press Manual setting. Cook at High Pressure for 8 minutes.
7. When done, quick-release pressure. Open lid carefully.
8. Press Sauté button. Cook until mixture thickens. Press Keep Warm/Cancel.
9. Serve.

Chapter 7: Side Dishes, Stocks, and Sauces

67. Ultimate Corn on the Cob

Time: 15 minutes

Servings: 4

Ingredients:

- 8 corn on the cob
- 2 cups of water
- 2 teaspoons low-carb brown sugar
- 1 teaspoon salt (to taste)
- 1 teaspoon fresh ground black pepper (to taste)

Instructions:

1. Pour 2 cups of water in Instant Pot.
2. Place corn in steamer basket. Place basket in Instant Pot.
3. Close and seal lid. Press Manual button. Cook at High Pressure for 5 minutes.
4. When timer beeps, naturally release pressure. Open lid carefully.
5. Sprinkle with brown sugar.
6. Serve.

68. Tangy Steamed Artichokes

Time: 25 minutes

Servings: 2

Ingredients:

- 2 artichokes
- Juice from 1 lemon
- 2 Tablespoons low-carb mayonnaise
- 2 cups of water
- 1 teaspoon paprika
- 1 teaspoon salt (to taste)
- 1 teaspoon fresh ground black pepper (to taste)

Instructions:

1. Wash and trim artichokes.
2. Pour 2 cups of water in Instant Pot.
3. Place artichokes in steamer basket. Place basket in Instant Pot.
4. Close and seal lid. Press Manual switch. Cook at High Pressure for 10 minutes.
5. When done, release pressure naturally. Open lid carefully.
6. In a bowl, combine mayonnaise, lemon juice, paprika, salt, and black pepper. Spread on artichokes.
7. Serve.

69. Succulent Sausage and Cheese Dip

Time: 10 minutes

Servings: 4

Ingredients:

- 1 pound ground Italian sausage

- ¼ cup green onions, chopped
- 1 cup cream cheese, softened
- 1 cup mozzarella cheese, shredded
- 1 cup cheddar cheese, shredded
- 1 cup vegetable broth
- 2 cups canned diced tomatoes
- 2 Tablespoons ghee, melted

Instructions:

1. Press Sauté button on Instant Pot. Heat the ghee.
2. Sauté Italian sausage and green onions, until sausage is brown.
3. Add remaining ingredients. Stir well.
4. Close and seal lid. Press Manual button. Cook at High Pressure for 5 minutes.
5. When timer beeps, naturally release pressure. Open lid carefully.
6. Serve.

70. Zesty Onion and Cauliflower Dip

Time: 20 minutes

Servings: 4

Ingredients:

- 1 head cauliflower, minced
- 1 cup chicken broth
- 1 ¼ cup low-carb mayonnaise
- 1 onion, chopped
- 1 cup cream cheese, softened
- 1 teaspoon Chili powder
- 1 teaspoon ground cumin
- 1 teaspoon garlic powder
- 1 teaspoon salt (to taste)

- 1 teaspoon fresh ground black pepper (to taste)

Instructions:

1. Add all ingredients to Instant Pot. Stir well.
2. Using a hand blender, blend ingredients.
3. Close and seal lid. Press Manual button. Cook at High Pressure for 10 minutes.
4. When timer beeps, naturally release pressure, Open lid carefully. Stir ingredients.
5. Serve.

71. Ravishing Mushrooms and Sausage Gravy

Time: 15 minutes

Servings: 4

Ingredients:

- 1 pound Italian ground sausage
- 2 Tablespoons coconut oil
- 1 yellow onion, diced
- 2 garlic cloves, minced
- 2 cups mushrooms, chopped
- 1 red bell pepper, minced
-
- 2 Tablespoons ghee, melted
- ⅓ cup coconut flour
- 3½ cups coconut milk, unsweetened
- ½ cup organic heavy cream
- 1 teaspoon salt (to taste)
- 1 teaspoon fresh ground black pepper (to taste)

Instructions:

1. Press Sauté button on Instant Pot. Heat the coconut oil.
2. Sauté onion and garlic for 2 minutes.
3. Add the Italian sausage. Cook until brown.
4. Add mushrooms, bell peppers. Sauté until soft. Season with salt and pepper.
5. Press Keep Warm/Cancel button to end Sauté mode.
6. In a small saucepan, over medium heat, melt the ghee. Add the flour. Whisk in coconut milk and heavy cream. Continue stirring until thickens.
7. Add flour mixture to Instant Pot. Stir well.
8. Close and seal lid. Press Manual button. Cook at High Pressure for 10 minutes.
9. When timer beeps, naturally release pressure. Open lid carefully.
10. Serve.

72. Flawless Cranberry Sauce

Time: 20 minutes

Servings: 4

Ingredients:

- 12-ounces fresh cranberries
- ¼ cup red wine
- 1 Tablespoon granulated Splenda
- Juice from 1 orange
- ⅛ teaspoon salt

Instructions:

1. Add all ingredients to Instant Pot. Stir well.
2. Close and seal lid. Press Manual switch. Cook at High Pressure for 2 minutes.
3. When timer beeps, naturally release pressure. Open lid carefully.

4. Crush the cranberries with a fork or masher. Stir again.
5. Serve warm or cold.

73. Perfect Marinara Sauce

Time: 15 minutes

Servings: 2

Ingredients:

- 2 (14-ounce) cans diced tomatoes
- 2 Tablespoons red wine vinegar
- ¼ cup coconut oil
- 1 teaspoon onion powder
- 1 teaspoon garlic powder
- 1 Tablespoon fresh oregano, chopped
- 1 Tablespoon fresh basil, chopped
- 1 Tablespoon fresh parsley, chopped
- 1 teaspoon salt
- 1 teaspoon fresh ground black pepper

Instructions:

1. Add the ingredients to Instant Pot. Stir well.
2. Close and seal lid. Press Manual button. Cook at High Pressure for 8 minutes.
3. When timer beeps, naturally release pressure. Open lid carefully.
4. Puree mixture with immersion blender.
5. Serve.

74. Very Cheesy Cheese Sauce

Time: 10 minutes

Servings: 2

Ingredients:

- 2 Tablespoons ghee
- ½ cup cream cheese, softened
- 1 cup cheddar cheese, grated
- 1 cup mozzarella cheese, grated
- 2 Tablespoons water (or coconut milk)
- ½ cup heavy whipping cream
- 1 teaspoon of salt

Instructions:

1. Press Sauté button on Instant Pot. Melt the ghee.
2. Add cream cheese, cheddar cheese, mozzarella cheese, water or/coconut milk, heavy whipping cream, and salt. Stir constantly until melted.
3. Press Keep Warm/Cancel button to end sauté mode.
4. Close and seal lid. Press Manual switch. Cook at High Pressure for 4 minutes.
5. When done, quick-release or naturally release pressure. Open lid carefully. Stir.
6. Serve.

75. Best Homemade Alfredo Sauce

Time: 15 minutes

Servings: 2

Ingredients:

- 1 cup coconut milk
- 2 cups Parmesan cheese, grated
- 1 onion, chopped

- 1 teaspoon of salt
- ½ lemon, juice
- ¼ cup + 1 Tablespoon nutritional yeast
- 2 Tablespoons ghee
- 1 teaspoon garlic powder
- 1 teaspoon ground nutmeg
- 1 teaspoon salt
- 1 teaspoon fresh ground black pepper

Instructions:

1. Press Sauté button on Instant Pot. Heat the ghee.
2. Sauté the garlic and onion until become translucent.
3. Add coconut milk, parmesan cheese, nutritional yeast, lemon juice, and seasonings. Stir constantly until smooth.
4. Press Keep Warm/Cancel button. Cook at High Pressure for 6 minutes.
5. When done, quick-release or naturally release pressure. Open lid carefully. Stir.
6. Serve.

76. Hot Dogs with a Twist

Time: 10 minutes

Servings: 4

Ingredients:

- 8 hot dogs
- 1 cup low-carb beer
- 8 ketogenic hot dog buns (for serving)

Instructions:

1. Place the hot dogs in Instant Pot.
2. Pour beer over the hot dogs.

3. Close and seal the lid. Press Manual button. Cook at High Pressure for 5 minutes;
4. When done, quick-release pressure. Open lid carefully.
5. Serve, on buns or alone.

77. Knockout Asparagus and Shrimp Mix

Time: 10 minutes

Servings: 4

Ingredients:

- 1 pound asparagus, trimmed and chopped
- 1 pound shrimp, peeled and deveined
- 2 Tablespoons ghee, melted
- 2 cups of water
- 1 teaspoon salt (to taste)
- 1 teaspoon fresh ground black pepper (to taste)

Instructions:

1. Pour 2 cups of water in Instant Pot.
2. Place shrimp and asparagus in steamer basket. Drizzle melted ghee over shrimp and asparagus. Season with salt and pepper. Place basket in Instant Pot.
3. Close and seal lid. Press Manual button. Cook at High Pressure for 6 minutes.
4. When timer beeps, release pressure naturally. Open lid carefully.
5. Serve.

78. Heavenly Stuffed Bell Peppers

Time: 30 minutes

Servings: 4

Ingredients:

- 1 pound lean ground beef
- 1 teaspoon coconut oil

- 4 medium to large bell peppers, de-seeded, tops sliced off
- 1 avocado, chopped
- Juice from 1 lime
- 1 jalapeno, minced (depending on heat level, remove or leave seeds)
- 2 green onions, chopped
- 2 cups of water
- 1 cup mixed cheeses, shredded
- 2 teaspoons chili powder
- 1 teaspoon garlic powder
- 1 teaspoon ground cumin
- 1 teaspoon salt (to taste)
- 1 teaspoon fresh ground black pepper (to taste)

Instructions:

1. Press Sauté button on Instant Pot. Heat the coconut oil.
2. Sauté ground beef until no longer pink; drain.
3. Place ground beef in a bowl. Add green onions, jalapeno, and seasoning. Stir well.
4. Stuff mixture in bell peppers.
5. Pour 2 cups of water in Instant Pot. Place stuffed peppers in steamer basket. Top with shredded cheese.
6. Close and seal lid. Press Manual button. Cook at High Pressure for 15 minutes.
7. When done, naturally release pressure. Open lid carefully.
8. Serve.

79. Delicious Broccoli and Garlic Combo

Time: 15 minutes

Servings: 4

Ingredients:

- 1 broccoli head, chopped into florets
- 2 Tablespoons coconut oil
- 6 garlic cloves, minced
- 2 cups of water
- 1 teaspoon salt (to taste)
- 1 teaspoon black pepper (to taste)

Instructions:

1. Press Sauté button on Instant Pot. Heat the coconut oil.
2. Sauté garlic for 2 minutes. Add the broccoli. Cook until softened. Set aside.
3. Press Keep Warm/Cancel button to end Sauté mode.
4. Pour 2 cups of water in Instant Pot. Place garlic and broccoli florets in steamer basket. Season with salt and black pepper.
5. Close and seal lid. Press Manual button. Cook at High Pressure for 10 minutes.
6. When done, naturally release pressure. Open lid carefully.
7. Transfer to a bowl. Stir well.
8. Serve.

80. Hollywood Collard Greens and Bacon

Time: 15 minutes

Servings: 4

Ingredients:

- 1 pound collard greens, trimmed and chopped
- ¼ pound bacon, chopped
- ½ cup ghee, melted
- 1 teaspoon salt
- 1 teaspoon fresh ground black pepper

Instructions:

1. Press Sauté button on Instant Pot. Melt 1 tablespoon of ghee.
2. Add the bacon. Sauté until bacon is brown and crispy.
3. Press Keep Warm/Cancel button to end Sauté mode.
4. Add collard greens, rest of the ghee, salt and pepper. Stir well.
5. Close and seal lid. Press Manual button. Cook at High Pressure for 10 minutes.
6. When done, naturally release pressure. Open lid carefully. Stir.
7. Serve.

81. Godly Kale Delish

Time: 15 minutes

Servings: 4

Ingredients:

- 1 bunch of kale, trimmed and chopped
- 1 red onion, thinly sliced
- 4 garlic cloves, minced

- 1 cup pine nuts, roughly chopped
- 1 cup vegetable broth
- 1 Tablespoon ghee, melted
- 2 Tablespoons coconut oil
- 1 Tablespoon balsamic vinegar
- 1 teaspoon red pepper flakes
- 1 teaspoon salt
- 1 teaspoon fresh ground black pepper

Instructions:

1. Press Sauté button on Instant Pot. Heat the coconut oil.
2. Sauté onion and garlic until they become translucent.
3. Press Keep Warm/Cancel button to end Sauté mode.
4. Add kale, pine nuts, melted ghee, balsamic vinegar, pine nuts, red pepper flakes, salt and pepper. Stir well.
5. Close and seal lid. Press Manual button. Cook at High Pressure for 8 minutes.
6. When done, quick-release pressure. Open lid carefully.
7. Adjust seasoning if needed.
8. Serve.

Chapter 8: Festival & Weekend Recipes

82. Authentic Indian Butter Chicken

Time: 25 minutes

Servings: 4

Ingredients:

- 4 chicken breasts, boneless, skinless
- 2 jalapeno peppers, chopped (remove seeds)
- 1 onion, chopped
- 4 garlic cloves, minced
- 1 cup heavy cream
- 2 teaspoons garam masala
- 1 cup Greek yogurt
- 2 Tablespoons cornstarch
- 2 Tablespoons chicken stock
- ¼ cup of fresh cilantro, chopped
- 2 (14-ounce) cans diced tomatoes
- 2 Tablespoons fresh ginger, grated
- ½ cup ghee, melted
- 2 Tablespoons coconut oil
- 2 teaspoons ground cumin
- 1 teaspoon cayenne pepper
- 1 teaspoon salt (to taste)
- 1 teaspoon fresh ground black pepper (to taste)

Instructions:

1. Rinse chicken, pat dry. Cut into chunks.
2. In a food processor, add canned tomatoes, ginger, jalapenos. Pulse until blended.
3. Press Sauté button on Instant Pot. Heat the coconut oil.

4. Sauté onion and garlic for 2 minutes, Add chicken breasts. Brown on all sides.
5. Press Keep Warm/Cancel button to stop Sauté mode.
6. Add rest of ingredients, including pureed tomato mixture. Stir well.
7. Close and seal lid. Press Manual button. Cook at High Pressure for 10 minutes.
8. When timer beeps, quick-release pressure. Open lid carefully. Stir well.
9. Serve.

83. Rockstar Chicken Wings

Time: 20 minutes

Servings: 4

Ingredients:

- 1 pound chicken wings
- 6 garlic cloves, minced
- 1 Tablespoon fresh ginger, grated
- 2 Tablespoons coconut oil
- 1 Tablespoon fresh rosemary, chopped
- 1 Tablespoon fresh thyme, chopped
- 1 teaspoon salt
- 1 teaspoon fresh ground black pepper
- 2 cups chicken broth

Instructions:

1. Drizzle coconut oil over chicken wings, turning so they are coated.
2. Season with ginger, rosemary, thyme, salt, and black pepper.
3. Press Sauté button on Instant Pot.
4. Sauté chicken wings until golden brown. Add garlic while cooking.
5. Press Keep Warm/cancel setting to end Sauté mode.
6. Add chicken broth.

7. Close and seal lid. Press Manual button. Cook at High Pressure for 8 minutes.
8. When timer beeps, naturally release pressure. Open lid carefully.
9. Serve.

84. Festive Okra Pilaf

Time: 25 minutes

Servings: 4

Ingredients:

- 1 pound okra, sliced
- 8 bacon slices, minced
- 2 cups cauliflower rice
- 1 cup tomatoes, minced
- 2 cups of water
- 1 Tablespoon ghee, melted
- 2 teaspoons paprika
- ¼ cup fresh cilantro, chopped
- 1 teaspoon salt
- 1 teaspoon fresh ground black pepper

Instructions:

1. Press Sauté button on Instant Pot.
2. Cook bacon until brown.
3. Sauté okra and cauliflower rice until softened.
4. Add remaining ingredients. Stir well.
5. Close and seal lid. Press Manual button. Cook at High Pressure for 10 minutes.
6. When done, quick-release pressure. Open lid carefully.
7. Serve.

Chapter 9: Special Occasion Recipes

85. Thankful Thanksgiving Whole Turkey

Time: 45 minutes

Servings: 6

Ingredients:

- 1 whole turkey (large enough for your Instant Pot)
- 1 Tablespoon fresh rosemary, chopped
- 1 Tablespoon fresh thyme, chopped
- 1 Tablespoon fresh sage, chopped
- 2 Tablespoons coconut oil
- 1 cup white wine vinegar
- 2 cups turkey or chicken broth
- 2 teaspoons onion powder
- 2 teaspoons garlic powder
- 2 teaspoons paprika
- 2 teaspoons salt
- 2 teaspoons fresh ground black pepper

Instructions:

1. Remove all parts in turkey cavity. Wash and pat dry.
2. Drizzle coconut oil over the turkey.
3. Combine seasoning and herbs. Rub all over surface of turkey.
4. Press Sauté button on Instant Pot.
5. Place turkey in Instant Pot. Sauté for 3 minutes; flip cook another 3 minutes. (Don't worry if parts of turkey are not golden brown.)
6. Press Keep Warm/Cancel setting to stop Sauté mode.
7. Pour white vinegar and broth over your turkey.
8. Close and seal lid. Press Manual switch. Cook at High Pressure for 30 minutes.
9. When timer beeps, naturally release pressure. Open lid carefully.

10.   Allow the turkey to rest for 5 minutes before removing.
11. Set turkey on a platter. Rest 20 minutes before slicing.
12. Serve.

86. Luscious Broccoli and Asparagus with Roasted Almonds

Time: 20 minutes

Servings: 4

Ingredients:

-   1 head broccoli, chopped into florets
-   1 pound asparagus, stemmed and chopped
-   4 garlic cloves, minced
-   1 cup almonds, chopped
-   2 Tablespoons coconut oil
-   1 shallot, thinly sliced
-   1 cup vegetable broth
-   ¼ cup fresh parsley, chopped
-   1 teaspoon salt (to taste)
-   1 teaspoon fresh ground black pepper (to taste)

Instructions:

1. Press Sauté mode on Instant Pot. Heat the coconut oil.
2. Sauté shallots and garlic for 2 minutes. Add broccoli florets and asparagus. Cook until vegetables soften.
3. Add remaining ingredients. Stir well.
4. Close and seal lid. Press Manual button. Cook on high pressure for 15 minutes.
5. Once done, quick-release pressure. Open lid carefully. Stir well.
6. Serve.

87. Yummy Mango Puree

Time: 20 minutes

Servings: 4

Ingredients:

- 2 mangos, chopped
- ¼ cup plump golden raisins
- 1 shallot, chopped
- 1 Tablespoon coconut oil
- 1 apple, cored and chopped
- 1 teaspoon cinnamon
- 2 Tablespoons fresh ginger, minced
- 1 cup granulated Splenda
- 1 Tablespoon apple cider vinegar
- 2 cups of water

Instructions:

1. Press Sauté button on Instant Pot. Heat the coconut oil.
2. Sauté shallot and ginger until translucent.
3. Press Keep Warm/Cancel button to cancel Sauté mode.
4. Add remaining ingredients. Stir well.
5. Close and seal lid. Press Manual button. Cook at High Pressure for 7 minutes.
6. When timer beeps, quick-release pressure. Open lid carefully. Stir ingredients.
7. Use immersion blender to blend ingredients until smooth.
8. Allow to cool in refrigerator.

88. Crunchy Pumpkin Pie

Time: 30 minutes

Servings: 6

Filling Ingredients:

- 3 cups pumpkin puree
- ½ cup granulated Splenda
- ½ cup coconut milk
- 2 teaspoons pumpkin pie spice
- 1 large egg

Crust Ingredients:

- 1 cup pecan cookies, crushed
- 1 cup toasted pecans, roughly chopped
- 2 Tablespoons ghee, melted

Instructions:

1. In a large bowl, combine pecan cookies and ghee.
2. In a separate bowl, combine filling ingredients.
3. Grease pie pan, suitable for Instant Pot, with non-stick cooking spray.
4. Press crust mixture into bottom of pan firmly.
5. Pour filling into crust. Top with toasted pecans. Cover with aluminum foil.
6. Pour 2 cups of water in Instant Pot. Place trivet in Pot. Place pie pan on the trivet.
7. Close and seal lid. Press Manual button. Cook at High Pressure for 15 minutes.
8. When timer beeps, naturally release pressure. Open lid carefully.
9. Cool for 30 minutes on counter. Refrigerate any uneaten portion.

Chapter 10: Amazing Desserts

89. Delectable Brownie Cake

Time: 25 minutes

Servings: 6

Ingredients:

- 4 Tablespoons butter, softened
- 2 eggs
- 1 cup of water
- ⅛ teaspoon salt
- ⅓ cup coconut flour (or almond meal)
- ⅓ cup cocoa powder, unsweetened
- ⅓ cup granulated Splenda
- ⅓ cup dark chocolate chips
- ⅓ cup chopped nuts (optional)

Instructions:

1. In a bowl, combine butter, eggs, water, coconut flour, cocoa powder, salt, and granulated Splenda. Stir well, but don't overmix.
2. Grease a 6-inch pan, suitable for Instant Pot, with non-stick cooking spray.
3. Pour brownie mixture in pan. Cover with aluminum foil.
4. Pour water in Instant Pot. Place a trivet inside. Place cake pan on trivet.
5. Close and seal lid. Press Manual button. Cook at High Pressure for 20 minutes.
6. When done, release pressure naturally. Open lid carefully.
7. Remove pan from Instant Pot. Allow to cool 15 minutes before slicing.

90. Healthy Corn Pudding

Time: 20 minutes

Servings: 4

Ingredients:

- 2 (14-ounce) cans of creamed corn
- 2 cups of water
- 2 cups coconut milk
- 2 Tablespoons granulated Splenda
- 2 large eggs
- 2 Tablespoons coconut flour
- ⅛ teaspoon salt
- 1 Tablespoon butter, softened

Instructions:

1. Pour 2 cups of water in Instant Pot. Place trivet inside.
2. Set to Simmer. Bring to a boil.
3. In a bowl, combine creamed corn, coconut milk, Splenda, eggs, coconut flour, salt, and butter. Stir well.
4. Grease a baking dish, suitable for Instant Pot, with non-stick cooking spray.
5. Pour corn mixture in baking dish. Cover with aluminum foil.
6. Place baking dish on trivet.
7. Close and seal lid. Press Manual button. Cook on High-Pressure for 20 minutes.
8. When done, quick release or naturally release pressure. Open lid carefully.
9. Remove corn pudding. Allow to cool before eating.

91. Lovely Cinnamon Baked Apples

Time: 10 minutes

Servings: 4

Ingredients:

- 6 apples, cored and sliced (or chopped)
- ½ cup plump golden raisins
- ½ cup nuts, chopped (your choice)
- 1 teaspoon pure cinnamon powder
- 3 packets raw stevia
- 1 teaspoon apple pie spice
- 3 Tablespoons butter, softened

Instructions:

1. In your Instant Pot, combine apples, raisins, nuts, cinnamon powder, stevia, apple pie spice, and butter. Stir well.
2. Close and seal lid. Press Manual button. Cook at High-Pressure for 10 minutes.
3. When done, release pressure naturally. Open lid carefully.
4. Serve.

92. Delicious Peach Cobbler

Time: 20 minutes

Servings: 4

Ingredients:

- 8 peaches, peeled and chopped
- 2 Tablespoons butter, softened
- ½ cup coconut flour
- 1 teaspoon vanilla extract
- ¼ cup granulated Splenda
- ¼ cup low-carb brown sugar
- 1 teaspoon pure cinnamon
- 1 teaspoon lime juice
- 1 cup coconut milk

Instructions:

1. In your Instant Pot, place peaches in single layer along bottom.
2. In a large bowl, combine coconut milk, butter, vanilla extract, coconut flour, brown sugar, and Splenda. Stir well. Pour mixture over peaches.
3. Close and seal lid. Press Manual button. Cook on High-Pressure for 10 minutes.
4. When done, release pressure naturally. Open lid carefully.
5. Spoon into bowls.

93. Creamy Chocolate Pudding

Time: 20 minutes

Servings: 2

Ingredients:

- 1 cup organic coconut milk
- 1½ cups organic heavy cream
- 2 Tablespoons cocoa powder, unsweetened
- ½ teaspoon stevia powder extract
- 1 Tablespoons raw, organic honey
- 8-ounce bittersweet dark chocolate, chopped
- 2 large eggs
- 2 Tablespoons butter, softened
- ⅓ cup coconut flour
- ¼ cup granulated Splenda
- ⅓ cup low-carb brown sugar
- 2 teaspoons vanilla extract
- ¼ teaspoon cinnamon
- ⅛ teaspoon salt
- 2 Tablespoons of water

Instructions:

1. In a saucepan, add coconut milk, heavy cream, cocoa powder, stevia powder extract, and honey. Stir well. Simmer 3 minutes.
2. Remove saucepan from heat. Add dark chocolate. Stir until melted. Set aside. Let it cool slightly before adding to rest of mixture.
3. In a large bowl, combine eggs, coconut flour, brown sugar, Splenda, vanilla extract, cinnamon, butter, and salt. Stir well.
4. Add chocolate mixture to batter. Stir well.
5. Pour 2 cups of water in Instant Pot. Place trivet inside.
6. Grease a pan, suitable for Instant Pot, with non-stick cooking spray.
7. Pour batter in pan. Cover with aluminum foil. Place on trivet.

8. Close and seal lid. Press Manual button. Cook at High-Pressure for 10 minutes.
9. When done, release pressure naturally. Open lid carefully.
10. Remove pan from Instant Pot. Allow to cool.
11. **Serve.**

94. Just as Filling Cauliflower Rice Pudding

Time: 20 minutes

Servings: 2

Ingredients:

- 1 head cauliflower
- 2 cups coconut milk
- 1 cup heavy cream
- 4 teaspoons cinnamon powder
- 1 teaspoon granulated Splenda
- 1 teaspoon pure stevia extract
- 1 teaspoon pure vanilla extract
- ½ teaspoon salt

Instructions:

1. Chop up cauliflower. Place pieces in food processor.
2. Pulse until cauliflower is rice-like consistency.
3. Pour cauliflower rice in Instant Pot.
4. Add coconut milk, cinnamon, Splenda, stevia extract, vanilla extract, and salt. Stir well.
5. Close and seal lid. Press Porridge button. Cook at High Pressure for 20 minutes.
6. When done, allow pressure to release naturally for 10 minutes.
7. After 10 minutes, press the Cancel button. Open lid carefully.
8. To finish off, add cream and vanilla extract. Stir well.

9. Serve in bowls.

95. Almost-Famous Chocolate Lava Cake

Time: 15 minutes

Servings: 4

Ingredients:

- ⅓ cup granulated Splenda
- 2 Tablespoons butter, softened
- ¼ cup coconut milk
- ¼ cup coconut flour (or any ketogenic alternatives)
- 1 large egg
- 1 Tablespoon cocoa powder, unsweetened
- Zest from ½ a lime
- ½ teaspoon baking powder
- ⅛ teaspoon salt
- 1 cup of water
- 4 ramekins

Instructions:

1. In a bowl, combine eggs, Splenda, butter, milk, coconut flour, egg, cocoa powder, lime zest, baking powder, and salt. Stir well.
2. Grease 4 ramekins with non-stick cooking spray.
3. Divide batter evenly in 4 ramekins.
4. Pour 2 cups of water in Instant Pot. Place trivet inside. Place ramekins on trivet.
5. Close and seal lid. Press Manual button. Cook at High-Pressure for 7 minutes.
6. When done, allow pressure to release naturally. Remove ramekins.
7. Allow lava cakes to cool 5 minutes.
8. Serve.

96. Irresistible Lemon Cheesecake

Time: 30 minutes (plus 6 hours for refrigerating)

Servings: 4

Ingredients:

- 1½ cups low-carb graham crackers (approximately 10-12 crackers)
- 2 teaspoons low-carb brown sugar
- 2 Tablespoons butter, melted
- 1 Tablespoon almond flour
- 1 package (16-ounce) cream cheese, softened
- ½ cup granulated sugar
- 1 teaspoon vanilla extract
- 2 large eggs
- ½ cup heavy whipping cream
- Zest and juice from 1 lemon

Instructions:

1. In a food processor, add graham crackers, brown sugar, and butter.
2. Pulse until well blended, almost sand-like consistency.
3. Grease a 6-inch cheesecake pan with non-stick cooking spray.
4. Press crust mixture into bottom of pan firmly.
5. Place in freezer for 10 minutes to harden.
6. In a separate bowl, combine cream cheese, granulated sugar, heavy cream, eggs, almond flour, zest and juice from lemon, and vanilla extract.
7. Stir vigorously or blend with hand mixer until smooth.
8. Pour filling over crust. Cover cheesecake pan with aluminum foil.
9. Pour 2 cups of water in Instant Pot. Place trivet inside. Place pan on trivet.
10. Close and seal lid. Press Manual button. Cook at High Pressure for 20 minutes.

11. Once done, naturally release pressure. Open lid carefully.
12. Allow cheesecake to rest in Instant Pot for 20 minutes.
13. Transfer cheesecake to refrigerator. Cool for 6 hours or overnight.
14. Top with whip cream and fresh lemon zest when serving.

97. Berry Bliss Cheesecake

Time: 30 minutes (plus 6 hours for refrigerating)

Servings: 4

Ingredients:

- 1½ cups low-carb graham crackers (approximately 10-12 crackers)
- 1 Tablespoon granulated Splenda
- 4 Tablespoons butter, melted
- 2 packages (16-ounce) cream cheese, softened:
- 1 cup granulated Splenda
- 3 large eggs
- ¼ cup sour cream
- Zest and juice from 1 lemon
- 1 teaspoon vanilla extract
- 1 cup heavy whipping cream
- 4 cups mixed fresh berries (keto-friendly, your choice)

Instructions:

1. Mash half the berries with a fork. Set aside.
2. In a food processor, add graham crackers, granulated Splenda, melted butter.
3. Pulse until sand-like consistency.
4. Grease 6-inch cheesecake pan, to fit Instant Pot, with non-stick cooking spray.

5. Press crust mixture into bottom of pan. Place in freezer 10 minutes to harden.
6. In a separate bowl, combine cream cheese, Splenda, eggs, sour cream, zest and juice from lemon, vanilla and heavy cream. Add crushed mixed berries.
7. Stir vigorously or blend with hand mixer until smooth.
8. Pour mixture over crust. Cover cheesecake pan with aluminum foil.
9. Pour 2 cups of water in Instant Pot. Place trivet inside. Place pan on trivet.
10. Close and seal lid. Press Manual button. Cook at High Pressure for 20 minutes.
11. Once done, naturally release pressure. Open lid carefully.
12. Allow cheesecake to rest for 20 minutes in Instant Pot.
13. Transfer cheesecake to refrigerator. Cool for 6 hours or overnight.
14. Top with rest of fresh berries when serving.

98. Fantastic Bread Pudding

Time: 25 minutes

Servings: 4

Ingredients:

- 6 slices low-carb day-old/stale bread, cut into cubes
- 1½ cups unsweetened almond milk
- 4 Tablespoons unsalted butter
- 3 large eggs
- ¼ cup granulated Splenda
- ¾ cup low-carb dark chocolate chips
- 1 teaspoon vanilla extract
- 1 cup plump golden raisins
- Zest from 1 lemon
- 2 cups of water

Instructions:

1. In a small bowl, combine eggs, Splenda and almond milk. Whisk until combined.
2. Melt the butter.
3. In a large bowl, add the bread. Pour melted butter over bread.
4. Add lemon zest, chocolate chips, and raisins.
5. Pour liquid mixture over bread. Stir well.
6. Grease baking dish, to fit Instant Pot, with non-stick cooking spray.
7. Pour in bread mixture. Cover with aluminum foil.
8. Pour 2 cups of water in Instant Pot. Place trivet inside. Place dish on trivet.
9. Close and seal lid. Press Manual button. Cook at High-Pressure for 20 minutes.
10. When done, release pressure naturally. Open lid carefully.
11. Allow bread pudding to rest 15 minutes in Instant Pot.
12. Serve.

Chapter 11: Wicked Recipes

99. Fabulous Goose Meat

Time: 30 minutes

Servings: 4

Ingredients:

- 4 goose breasts, boneless, skinless (or any other goose meat)
- 1 (12-ounce) can cream of mushroom soup
- 2 Tablespoons coconut oil
- 1 teaspoon garlic powder
- 1 teaspoon onion powder
- 1 teaspoon paprika
- 2 teaspoons salt
- 2 teaspoons fresh ground black pepper

Instructions:

1. Press Sauté button on Instant Pot. Heat the coconut oil.
2. Sauté goose meat until golden brown crust per side.
3. Press Keep Warm/Cancel button to end Sauté mode.
4. In a small bowl, combine the spices. Sprinkle the seasoning over the goose.
5. Pour cream of mushroom soup over meat.
6. Close and seal lid. Press Manual button. Cook at High Pressure for 10 minutes.
7. When timer beeps, naturally release pressure. Open lid carefully.
8. Allow dish to rest 5 minutes before removing from Instant Pot.
9. Serve.

100. Nourishing Jambalaya

Time: 15 minutes

Servings: 4

Ingredients:

- 1 pound chicken breasts, boneless, skinless
- 1 pound Italian sausage
- 2 Tablespoons coconut oil
- 1 red onion, chopped
- 2 garlic cloves, minced
- 2 cups cauliflower rice
- 2 bell peppers, chopped
- 2 cups crushed tomatoes
- 1 Tablespoon Worcestershire sauce
- 3 cups chicken broth
- 1 teaspoon salt (to taste)
- 1 teaspoon fresh ground black pepper (to taste)

Instructions:

1. Rinse the chicken, pat dry. Chop into bite-size pieces.
2. Slice Italian sausage into circles, ¼ inch thick.
3. Press Sauté button on Instant Pot. Heat the coconut oil
4. Sauté red onion and garlic for 2 minutes.
5. Add chicken and Italian sausage. Sauté until meat is brown.
6. Press Keep Warm/Cancel to end Sauté mode.
7. Add cauliflower rice, bell peppers, crushed tomatoes. Stir well.
8. Stir in chicken broth, Worcestershire sauce, salt and pepper.
9. Close and seal lid. Press Manual button. Cook at High Pressure for 10 minutes.
10. When done, quick-release pressure. Open lid carefully. Serve.

101. Party Octopus

Time: 20 minutes

Servings: 4

Ingredients:

- 1 octopus, cleaned
- 2 Tablespoons ghee, melted
- Juice from ½ lemon
- 1 Tablespoon fresh rosemary, chopped
- 1 Tablespoon fresh oregano, chopped
- 1 Tablespoon of fresh thyme, chopped
- 1 teaspoon garlic powder
- 1 teaspoon onion powder
- 1 teaspoon salt
- 1 teaspoon fresh ground black pepper
- 2 cups of water

Instructions:

1. Place octopus in Instant Pot.
2. Add melted ghee, water, lemon juice, herbs, and seasonings. Stir well.
3. Close and seal lid. Pres Manual button. Cook at High Pressure for 15 minutes.
4. When timer beeps, naturally release pressure. Open lid carefully.
5. Serve.

Chapter 12: 14-Day Meal Plan for Rapid Fat Loss

In this chapter, we will provide you with an effective 14-day ketogenic meal plan. The main goal of the Ketogenic diet is to keep your daily carbohydrate intake under 100 grams - meaning you should consume between 20 to 100 grams of carbs in a day.For this diet plan, consuming under 100 grams should be easy for you to adapt. However, feel free to alter anything on the list depending on your preferences.

(Note: When searching for a recipe, please refer to the Table of Contents at the beginning of the book. This is just a sample of what a 14-day meal plan could be for you. Feel free to adjust the meal plan or substituting a ketogenic-friendly option.)

Day One

Breakfast: Deluxe Cauliflower Stew

Lunch: Lovely Tilapia Fillets

Dinner: Gratifying Meatloaf

Day Two

Breakfast: Weeknight Clam Chowder

Lunch: Scrumptious Brussel Sprouts

Dinner: Lavender Pork Chops

Day Three

Breakfast: Appetizing Steamed Crab Legs

Lunch: Magnificent Asparagus Stew

Dinner: Smoky Bacon Chili

Day Four

Breakfast: Hollywood Collard Greens and Bacon

Lunch: Knockout Asparagus and Shrimp Mix

Dinner: Contest-Winning Lamb Curry

Day Five

Breakfast: Hot Dogs with a Twist

Lunch: Heavenly Stuffed Bell Peppers

Dinner: Juicy Brisket

Day Six

Breakfast: Tangy Steamed Artichokes

Lunch: Rockstar Chicken Wings

Dinner: Melt-In-Your-Mouth Salisbury Steak

Day Seven

Breakfast: Fantastic Chili Lime Cod

Lunch: Splendid Broccoli and Ham Chowder

Dinner: Flavorsome Pulled Pork

Day Eight

Breakfast: Buddha's Tofu and Broccoli Delight

Lunch: Appetizing Steamed Crab Legs

Dinner: Wondrous Mediterranean Fish

Day Nine

Breakfast: Fragrant Zucchini Mix

Lunch: Awesome Vegan Patties

Dinner: Authentic Indian Butter Chicken

Day Ten

Breakfast: Generous Orange Trout Fillets

Lunch: Tongue Kicking Jalapeno Popper Soup

Dinner: Killer Baby Back Ribs

Day Eleven

Breakfast: Everyday Bold Beet and Caper Salad

Lunch: Super Yummy Pork Chops

Dinner: Stunning Shrimp and Sausage Gumbo

Day Twelve

Breakfast: Enriching Lamb Stew

Lunch: Lovely Ginger Beef and Kale

Dinner: Extraordinary Pork Roast

Day Thirteen

Breakfast: Intriguing Oysters

Lunch: Wonderful Eggplant Lasagna

Dinner: Festive Okra Pilaf

Day Fourteen

Breakfast: Delicious Broccoli and Garlic Mix Combo

Lunch: Godly Kale Delish

Dinner: Fabulous Goose Meat

Conclusion

Thank you very much for choosing this keto diet Instant Pot Cookbook!

After reading this book, you should know what the ketogenic diet is, why it is good for you, how to follow the ketogenic diet. You are now prepared to embark on the Ketogenic Lifestyle with 101 recipes using your Instant Pot. You also have at your fingertips a sample meal plan and tips for maintaining the ketogenic diet.

Lastly, if you enjoyed this book, please take the time to review it on Amazon. Your honest feedback would be greatly appreciated. Thank you, and the best of blessings on your Ketogenic journey.

Made in the USA
Lexington, KY
06 January 2018